Neil Van Heer
Grade 5

D0324415

TEACH ME THY WAY

Written by

J. MARION SNAPPER, Ed.D.
Department of Education, Calvin College
GORDON J. SPYKMAN, Th.D.
Department of Bible, Calvin College

Illustrated by
NORMAN MATHEIS

Produced by
The Committee on Education of the
Christian Reformed Church
The Reverend WILLIAM VANDER HAAK, Editor
Grand Rapids, Michigan

Printed in the United States of America

CONTENTS

PHOTO CREDITS—Harold M. Lambert Studios p. 16, 95, 160; A. Devaney, Inc. p. 24, (David W. Corson p. 127), 128, 145, 161; Eva Luoma p. 104, 109; H. Armstrong Roberts p. 140; Robert Brouwer p. 162, 163, 166, 171; W. Vander Haak p. 172; Religious News Service p. 175.

INTRODUCING A FRIEND

Good books are good friends. We hope that this book will become one of your best friends.

A friend is someone you like to have close to you, someone you treat kindly, someone who helps you along the way.

We hope this book will become that kind of good friend to you.

If you make this book your friend, then it will help you understand better the meaning of that favorite hymn, "What a Friend we have in Jesus." This book as your friend will take you by the hand and lead you to the very best Friend of all, Jesus.

Why is Jesus our very best Friend? Because He teaches us the way to live as Christians and helps us along the road of Christian living.

So whenever you use this book, think of your life as a trip. As you travel along, Jesus is your Guide and God's Word is your Map. Think of this book then as a series of friendly signs along the way, pointing you in the right direction and helping you keep your eye on the right road ahead.

You know what happens if you miss a highway sign. You lose your way, and lose time, and sometimes get lost. Every good traveller knows that he must watch the traffic signs. Remember that as you use this book. Each lesson is a travelling sign. Study all the signs carefully. Then you will learn to live as a Christian with Christ as your Guide and the Bible as your Map.

Now you see why this book has the title, *Teach Me Thy Way*. It gives Christian boys and girls travelling tips for life. This idea of your life as a trip will come up many times in this book, especially in the four review lessons. Keep this in mind.

As you move along, there are many travelling tunes to sing. But make this your theme song:

> *Teach me, o Lord, Thy way of truth,*
> *And from it I will not depart;*
> *That I may steadfastly obey,*
> *Give me an understanding heart.*

Lesson 1

HOW GOD GAVE US THE BIBLE

Your first lesson for this year is about the Bible. You have read the Bible and you probably have your own copy. This week you will study the important and interesting story of how God gave His Word to man, and how the Bible has come down to us in the twentieth century.

When you go to the library to pick out a book to read, you probably keep your eye open for a new one—one you haven't seen before. There are hundreds of new books printed every year. But do you know that one of the oldest books in the world is also the best-selling Book? If all of the copies of that Book that were sold or given away in a single year were put in one stack, the pile would reach higher than the orbit of the astronauts who circle the earth. That Book is the Bible.

How is the Bible different from all other books?

Among all the books in the world the Bible is a very special one. All other books are the words of men. The Bible is the Word of God. There is no other book like it. For in the Bible God speaks to us through men like Moses and David, Matthew and Paul. He tells about Himself, about ourselves, about our world, about sin, about salvation through Jesus Christ, and about how we must live as Christians.

As you read the Bible and listen to it, have you ever wondered just how that wonderful Book came into being? How God gave it? How it came down through hundreds and hundreds of years to us? This is a very interesting story. To understand it we must go back in our thoughts to the time of Jesus and the apostles, to the time of the Old Testament prophets and kings, and even farther back to the time of Moses and Abraham.

> *The Bible is sometimes called The Book.*
> *It could just as well be called The Library.*
> *Why is this so?*

The Moslems believe that their book, the Koran, was given by an angel to one man. But this is not how God gave us the Bible. God used about forty different men to write the Bible. More than two thousand years ago God spoke to Moses and he wrote the first five books of the Bible. Many years later God spoke to such men as Samuel the prophet, David the king, and they wrote parts of the Bible too. Then there were the sixteen prophets who wrote books that became a part of the Bible. When Jesus came into the world, the thirty-nine books of the Old Testament were already there. After Jesus returned to heaven, apostles and disciples wrote the twenty-seven books of the New Testament. Thus, for hundreds of years, God was revealing Himself to men. One after another we got the sixty-six books that are found in your Bible.

> *What are four ways in which God*
> *revealed Himself to the writers of*
> *the Bible?*

The authors of these Bible books wrote what God revealed to them. God revealed many things to them. And God revealed these things in different ways.

Sometimes God revealed Himself through wonderful things that they could *see*. For example, in the Old Testament God spoke to Moses in the burning bush. And in the New Testament He spoke to Paul in the shining light from heaven when he was on the road to Damascus.

At other times God revealed Himself directly through words that they could *hear*. For example, in the Old Testament He spoke to the boy Samuel at night in the tabernacle. And in the New Testament He spoke from heaven at the baptism of Jesus in the Jordan River.

God also revealed Himself in the wonderful way He took care of His people. He sometimes used *miracles*. For example, in the Old Testament God used the Red Sea crossing to show that He had chosen Israel as His special nation. And in the New Testament He showed His power by raising Lazarus from the dead.

But God's greatest revelation came to us in *Jesus Christ*. Christ is God's greatest revelation. In Jesus men could hear God speaking. In Jesus men could see God working.

Why did God have men put down in
books what He revealed to them?

What if all these things had never been written in a Book? They might have been forgotten. Surely they would have been changed. You know how a story can change after it has been told many times by different people. If that had happened, we would never know for sure what God revealed to us about Himself. That is why God chose all those different men from different times to write what they had seen and heard. In this way His Word could be saved for all people to read.

How did God guide those men as they
wrote what is in the Bible?

As the Bible authors wrote, God guided them by His Holy Spirit so that they wrote what He wanted them to write. But each writer was different, and God used the thoughts, the words and the experiences of each man. As you read the Bible

The scroll of Isaiah, from the Dead Sea Scrolls, opened to chapter 40. The scroll is 24 feet long. By permission of the American School of Oriental Research.

you can tell that the different books were written by different men. For example, if you read the writings of Amos you can tell that he was a farmer. He uses such examples as "plowing on rocks" and "baskets of fruit." But even though each one wrote in his own way, he wrote just what God wanted him to say. These writers did not write everything about God. They put down those things that God knew we would need in order to know Him, to believe in Him, and to be good Christians.

Many other books were also written during the Old and New Testament times. But only those that were written in the way described here were included in our Bible. That is why the Bible is the best Book of all.

How did we get our Bible in English?

There was one more problem. The Old Testament was written in the Hebrew language and the New Testament in the Greek language. These languages looked like this:

Psalm 23:1a מִזְמוֹר לְדָוִד יְהוָה רֹעִי לֹא אֶחְסָר׃ ²בִּנְאוֹת דֶּשֶׁא יַרְבִּיצֵנִי

John 3:16a οὕτως γὰρ ἠγάπησεν ὁ θεὸς τὸν κόσ

Can you understand or read these languages? Well, other people couldn't read them either. So the Bible had to be translated into many languages, because God's Word was meant to be understood by everyone. Today the Bible has been translated into more than one thousand languages, such as Latin, French, German, Dutch and Spanish. In the English language we have many different translations, such as the King James Version, the American Standard Version, and the Revised Standard Version.

Abraham Lincoln said, "I believe the Bible is the best gift God has ever given to man. All the good from the Saviour of the world is communicated to us through this Book." We should be thankful to God for giving us the Bible and putting it into our hands in our own language.

God speaks to us in the Bible just as surely as our parents speak to us. In the words of the boy Samuel you should now answer, "Speak, for thy servant heareth" (I Samuel 3:10).

PRAYER

Dear Father in heaven, I praise and thank Thee for the Book that never lies to me, for the one Book that I can really trust. I thank Thee for the Book that tells me about Thee and shows me Thy love in sending Jesus Christ to die for my sins. I thank Thee for the Book that teaches me how to live as a Christian. I thank Thee for the Bible. Teach me to listen to Thy voice as it speaks to me in my Bible, and to be obedient to Thy Word. For Jesus' sake, Amen.

BIBLE VERSE

For no prophecy ever came by the will of man: but men spake from God, being moved by the Holy Spirit.
II Peter 1:21

THINKING IN BLACK-ON-WHITE

1. How many books are there in the Old Testament? In the New Testament? How many are there in the whole Bible?

2. In what languages was the Bible first written?

3. If someone asked you, "What makes the Bible different from every other book?" what would you answer? Look up II Timothy 3:16, 17 and II Peter 1:21.

4. Which of the following sentences best describes how God gave the Bible to man? Choose the answer you think is best.

   a. God gave the Bible ready-made and all-at-once from heaven.

   b. The men who wrote the Bible put down what they thought about God.

c. God's Holy Spirit directed the men in what they wrote, so that, using their own words, they wrote exactly what God wanted written.

d. God helped the men who wrote the Bible, just as He helps a minister today who prays for help in writing a sermon.

(If you are asked in class, be able to explain what you believe is wrong with the sentences you didn't choose.)

5. Mention four different ways in which God revealed Himself to the authors of the Bible.

6. Why did God have men put in writing what He revealed to them? Read Revelation 1:19 and 21:5.

7. The Bible you use is a translation. What does that mean?

QUESTIONS AND ANSWERS FOR MEMORY WORK

1. **Who wrote the Bible?**

The Bible was written by many men, starting with Moses centuries before Jesus came, and ending with John after Jesus returned to heaven.

2. **How did God reveal Himself to the Bible authors?**

God revealed Himself in ways that men could see and hear, and through miracles, but especially in His Son, Jesus Christ.

3. **How did God guide the writing of the Bible?**

God guided the writing of the Bible by allowing each writer to use his own thoughts, words and experiences in such a way that what they wrote was the Word of God.

4. **Why was the Bible translated from Hebrew and Greek into our language?**

The Bible was translated into our language so that we could "search the scriptures" (John 5:39) to understand God's messages to us.

WHAT DO YOU THINK ABOUT IT?

1. While on vacation in New Mexico Peter went to a rodeo. Somehow he and his younger brother wandered away from their parents. Suddenly they found themselves in the path of four stampeding steers. Quickly Peter pulled his brother through a fence to a safe place. It was a narrow escape! Back home in Chicago, Peter told this exciting story over and over again. But each time he changed the story and added things to show what a great hero he was. This often happens when news is repeated. Then we lose the truth. Now, what if the mighty works of Jesus had never been written down, but had been only told and retold for two thousand years? Could we be sure about the truth?

2. When men first started translating the Bible into the English language, they were persecuted for doing this. The leaders didn't want the people to be able to read the Bible. Why was this wrong?

GOD'S GREAT LOVE TO US

Last week we learned about the Book that God gave us. The most wonderful truth the Bible teaches us is that "God is love" (I John 4:8). God loves us because He made us. He loves the whole world that He created. Even after sin came into the world, God loved us so much that He sent His Son into the world to save us from our sins. If you want to see the greatness of God's love, look at Jesus Christ. The Bible does not tell us what love is in the way a dictionary does. It tells us the story of God and what He has done for His world and His people through Jesus Christ.

The word "Gospel" means "good news."
Why is the Gospel God's "good news" to us?

One of our very best friends is the mailman. We like him because he brings us letters. Everybody likes to receive letters, especially if they bring good news.

That is why Christians love the Bible. For the Bible is like a letter from our heavenly Father. It brings good news. It is God's love letter to us, because it tells about God's great love for us. Of course, the Bible tells us many other things about God too. It tells of His greatness, power and holiness. These

things make us feel humble. But the best news in the Bible is about God's goodness and love. That news makes us feel happy.

What is love?

Everyone of us knows something about love. We use the word so much. We say that father and mother love each other. Ladies sometimes say, "I just love that dress you are wearing." Boys say, "I would love to have a new basketball." We have all sung that little song, "Jesus loves me, this I know, for the Bible tells me so." What do you think it means that Jesus loves you? What do you think it means that God so loved the world that He gave us His Son?

Can you say what love means? That is very hard to do, isn't it? Is it just being nice to someone? Did someone ever say to you, "Now you be nice to them when they are visiting us. I know you don't like them, but just be nice while they are here"? So you see, just because we try to be nice to people doesn't mean that we love them.

How shall we find out what love really means? There is just one way. That is by seeing how God loves, because God *is* love. All real love comes from God. And even though we use the word *love* in many ways, we have to look to God's love to find out what it really means.

We can learn about real love only by seeing that God is love, and by seeing how God loves.

God's love is a holy love, a strong love, a perfect love. It is the greatest and purest love in the whole universe. God is the only One who knows how to love in a perfect way. Let us look at the beautiful and perfect love of God. You can see it best in the way He has shown His love to you. When you look at the love of God, what do you see?

Do you see this? God loves me so much that, even though I have done bad things, He has done only good things for me. I have broken His laws and have done so many things to make Him angry. But He doesn't punish me. Instead He gives me the best gift of all. He sent His Son to die for all the wrong things I do. When my classmates do things that I don't like, I don't want to have anything to do with them. But even when I do things that God doesn't like, He keeps on loving me, and tries to help me be better.

What difference is there between our love for others and God's love for us?

Let's be honest with ourselves. We don't love the way God loves, do we? At least, we don't love that way all of the time. Don't you find it hard to love some people? Brothers and sisters sometimes scream at each other, "I hate you!" Sometimes we show that we don't like people of another race or color or nation. Playmates are often very unkind to each other.

Oh, yes, it's easy enough to say, "I love everybody." But what about that bully down the street or that nasty girl around the corner? Do you really love your enemies, as Jesus commanded? When we talk about our enemies we often say, "They don't deserve to be loved!"

Do you remember what we have said about the way God

loves us? We don't deserve to be loved either. We have sinned. We couldn't expect God to love us any more. But He did. He sent His Son, Jesus Christ, to take away our sins. He changed our hearts and lives. He made us His friends. Even though we were just like naughty children who run away from home, He adopted us back into His family.

Only the love of God could do all this for us. Our minds cannot understand the greatness of this love. But we can receive it. Our love cannot equal God's love. But we can imitate it in our thoughts and words and deeds.

We can find many examples and illustrations of God's love in our lives.

Let's mention some more ways in which God loves us. He made us in His likeness. He created this wonderful world as our home. He takes care of plants and animals and birds. He controls the sun and moon, rain and sunshine, winter and summer. He gives us our daily bread. He gives us strength for work and play, and peaceful nights for restful sleep. He makes us well in times of sickness. He comforts us when we are sad. He hears our prayers. He forgives our sins. Even to wicked men He gives the good things of life. He sends the message of love even to His enemies.

Sometimes God's love works in surprising and unpleasant ways. When we are disobedient He disciplines us. Does this seem like love to you? It really is, for God disciplines us just because He loves us. He always seeks what is best for us.

Sometimes it takes things that hurt to make us what we ought to be. But behind this we should always look for God's hand of love, trying to make us better Christians. When God sends hard things into our lives, He is treating us much like our good parents do when they discipline us in order to make us better children. One thing is forever sure—you need never worry about God's goodness. He will never let you get beyond His loving care.

Love is never a one-way street.

As you know, on a one-way street all traffic flows in the same direction. Some people think of God's love that way. They expect God to love them, and they want God to be good to them. But they never return these favors. They fail to answer God's love. This is very selfish and unthankful. Love must come from both sides. We must love God because He first loved us.

Now let's face this question: Whom do you love most of all? Your parents? Your brothers and sisters? Your friends? Or yourself? Often we find ourselves loving all the good things God gives us, but forgetting to love God who is the Giver of them all. At such times this reminder is necessary—our love must reach higher than people and things. We must love God above everything else. He is worthy of our love, for He is love and He never keeps that love to Himself. He always shares it with us.

This is the Gospel, the greatest good news in all the world! We have this love story in a nutshell in the parable of the father and his runaway boy. Really it is a story about our heavenly Father and us, His children. Read this exciting story in Luke 15:11-32, and then thank God for His great love for you. Then, if you are wondering how you can show your love to God, read the first letter of John in the Bible. It is a short letter and it is all about love. In short, here is the answer to your question: "For this is the love of God, that we keep his commandments" (I John 5:3).

Finally, pray the prayer that follows, and try to live what you ask for in this prayer.

PRAYER

O God of love, teach us about Thy love so that we may thank Thee for all Thy goodness to us. We cannot measure the greatness of Thy love, but we accept it by faith.

Help us to be "living letters" of love, loving Thee above all and loving our neighbors as ourselves, so that other people may see the love of God shining from our lives. In Jesus' name, Amen.

BIBLE VERSE

Behold what manner of love the Father hath bestowed upon us, that we should be called children of God; and such we are. —I John 3:1

THINKING IN BLACK-ON-WHITE

1. Why do we call the Bible the Gospel, that is, the Book of God's "good news" to us? Read Luke 2:10, 11.

2. Describe in which ways God's love is greater than our love.

3. Explain this statement: "We love God because he first loved us." See I John 4:19.

4. Mention some ways in which God shows His great love to us.

5. How should we show our love to God?

QUESTIONS AND ANSWERS FOR MEMORY WORK

1. **What does the Bible teach you about God's love?**

   The Bible teaches me that "God is love" (I John 4:8), and therefore "every good gift and every perfect gift is from above" (James 1:17).

2. **What are the main ways in which God shows His love to you?**

   God shows His love to me in creating me in His likeness, in caring for my daily needs, and in saving me from my sins.

3. **How must you answer God's love in your daily living?**

   I must answer God's love in my daily living by loving God above all and loving my neighbors as I love myself (Matthew 22:37-39).

WHAT DO YOU THINK ABOUT IT?

1. A boy in class once asked his minister this question: "Is it really true, as you say, that my dad spanks me because he loves me?" "Yes, Jack, that's right," replied the minister. "Wow!" answered Jack, "my dad sure must love me!"

   His answer made the class laugh. But what can we learn from this story about Jack and his father that will help us understand how God our Father sometimes treats us?

2. Looking up from the game they were playing, Ruth and Harriet watched the movers carrying furniture into a house across the street. A new family was moving into the neighborhood. They had a girl about ten years old. This is what the girls said:

   Harriet: I don't like her 'cause she's got dark-colored skin.

   Ruth: My mother says they've got a strange-sounding name too.

   Harriet: I'm not going to invite her to my party.

   Ruth: Let's not even play with her.

   If you were a friend of Ruth and Harriet, what would you say about this?

THE PLAN OF CREATION

We live in an age of great discoveries. Our ideas about the world are changing all the time. With the invention of air and space travel, our earth seems to be getting smaller and our universe larger. We are finding out more and more about the wonders of God's great creation. We keep looking forward to new things. But to see how it all got started, we must look back to God's work in the beginning. Only the Bible can tell us about this. Genesis 1 and 2 teaches us that God created the world according to a good and wise plan. That is why life got started in an orderly way and men can still make progress today. As we see this plan of creation, we should praise God as the Creator.

Man is a great builder, but God is the greatest Builder.

There is a powerful song called "The Builder" by James W. Foley. The first verse pictures man the builder. The second verse praises God the Builder. Read the words carefully:

I am the builder of castle and hall
And I lay the stone in the temple wall;
I lay the stone and I raise the tower,
And mine is the glory of strength and power;
For I am the builder.

I am the Builder of forest and glade,
I am the Hand that has hewn and made
The peak of the mountains, the caves of the sea,
I am the Maker of worlds that be.

It all began with God.

IN THE BEGINNING GOD . . .

To understand God's plan in building the world we must go back in our thoughts to the very beginning. There was once a time when only God existed. There was no earth, no sun, no planets, no Milky Ways, no galaxies whirling through space obeying the laws of gravity. There were no plants, no animals, no people. There was only God. It is through Him that everything got started.

The world began as an idea in the mind of God. It was a wonderful idea, a great plan. Then, in the beginning, God began to work out this plan of creation. Out of nothing He created the heavens and the earth. The writer of Genesis pictures it as though he were there as an on-the-spot reporter watching God at work creating one thing after another.

God is not only a Builder, but He is first of all a Planner. How does the story of creation reveal God's great plan?

If you try hard, you can almost see it happening in your imagination. The time came when God decided to put His plan into action. In an orderly way God went to work to make His wonderful ideas become real. Step by step, day by day He moved ahead. God didn't make everything all at once. He

didn't finish His plan of creation in one great act. Instead, He took six days to do it, piece by piece, until it was complete.

Like a fine artist painting a picture, God added one stroke after another and blended one color after another until the beautiful picture was perfect. That is why He called it "very good" (Genesis 1:31). Like a wise builder, God drew one line after another and worked out one drawing after another until the building was finished. God is the great Builder, the great Planner.

The world didn't just happen by chance, but was created according to the plan of God.

We all understand how important it is to plan carefully. When you build a model airplane you first study the instructions carefully. When you help your mother bake a cake you follow the recipe. A carpenter builds a house according to a blueprint. In order to do a thing well we must first carefully plan it. A new church building takes months of planning. To launch a rocket takes years of planning.

The creation of the world was also the result of God's careful planning. It didn't just happen by accident. It didn't come by chance. It was not the result of magic. It didn't just grow up by itself. God worked it out in an orderly way. Then when the six days were over, there it was—God's plan come true!

There are two main steps in God's plan of creation. Think of it this way: step one—"the plaster"; step two—"the model."

Pretend you are making a plaster model. There are really two big steps in this job. *First* you must mix the plaster. *Then* you can shape the plaster into whatever you want to make.

God worked something like this. Only He had to start with nothing. Out of nothing He *first* created the stuff to use in making the world, such things as air and water and sand and heat and minerals and a lot of other things. But this didn't look much like a world. It was a pile of materials to work out His plan. *Then* He moved ahead. One day He sent light into this dark, mixed-up stuff. Another day He divided the sky above from the earth below. Another day He separated the land from the sea. He made day and night. He created plants and animals and birds. When everything else was ready, He created man.

God never works in a helter-skelter way. He plans things carefully. Then He works them out in an orderly way. We see this in the one-two-three-four-five-six steps that God followed when He created the world in six days.

6 + 1 = 7

There is a time for work and a time for rest. God included both work and rest in His plan for creation and in His plan for our lives.

We have seen how God put His plan into action. Out of nothing He brought forth everything that is in the world. He did this in six days. Then came the seventh day. That day is

like our Sunday. On that day God rested from His work of creation. Everything was ready. And God was happy.

All this happened long ago. But even today God wants us to follow His pattern in our lives. Six days we work for Him. On the seventh day we rest from our work in order to worship Him. You see, six plus one always equals seven. And that's the way our week goes.

PRAYER

O God, Planner and Maker of the world, we honor Thee for Thy wonderful creation. We thank Thee for giving us a place in Thy great plan for the world. Open our eyes to see Thy power and beauty. Open our hearts to worship Thee for Thy greatness and goodness. Open our mouths to praise Thee forever. Help us to use all our days for work and worship unto Thy glory. For Jesus' sake, Amen.

BIBLE VERSE

Jehovah by wisdom founded the earth;
By understanding he established the heavens.

Proverbs 3:19

THINKING IN BLACK-ON-WHITE

1. Why is it very important in this age of great discoveries to know what the Bible tells us about creation?
2. Compare man as a builder with God the Builder. Read again the poem at the beginning of the lesson.
3. Why is God the only Person who can tell us how the world started?
4. How does Genesis 1 and 2 show that God was working according to a wise plan in creating the world?
5. What do you think about the idea that the world just happened to get started by accident or chance? See Psalm 24:1, 2 and Psalm 33:6.

6. What were the two main steps God followed in His work of creation?

7. How can we see God's plan of creation still at work in the way we use the seven days of the week?

QUESTIONS AND ANSWERS FOR MEMORY WORK

1. **WHO created the world?**
The world was created by our heavenly Father who is both our Maker and our Savior.

2. **HOW did the world begin?**
The world began not by accident or chance, but according to the good and wise plan of God.

3. **WHAT can you learn from God's use of the days of creation?**
I can learn from the six days of creation and the seventh day of rest that I also must use six days for work and one day for rest and worship.

WHAT DO YOU THINK ABOUT IT?

1. Gordon Cooper was one of the first astronauts to circle the earth in his space ship. While he was in orbit he spoke this prayer:

   "Father, thank You, especially for letting me fly this flight. Thank You for the privilege of being able to be in this position: to be up in this wondrous place, seeing all these many startling, wonderful things that You have created."

   What do you think made Gordon Cooper want to pray?

2. Stanley came running over to Bob's house. "Sunday my cousin Tom is coming," he panted, "and we're going to build a tree-house! Bring your dad's hammer and you can help us." If you were Bob, what would your answer be?

GOD'S PLAN FOR OUR LIVES

In our last lesson we saw that God had a plan for creation. In this lesson we shall see that God also has a plan for our lives— for your life today. We shall learn how you can know God's will for your life.

What has God been doing since He finished creating the world?

The Bible tells us that God created the world in six days and rested on the seventh day. Does this mean that after God finished His work of creation He has been taking a long vacation? Does this mean that God has been without work for thousands of years? Is God's creation something like a clock that He wound up and that continues running, while God sits back and takes a rest?

CREATION

This cannot be so. For Jesus once said, "My Father worketh even until now, and I work" (John 5:17). When the Bible says that God rested on the seventh day, it means that He rested from His work of creation. He turned from this kind of work to another kind of work. After God made the world, the plants and animals and people, He didn't forget about them and leave them alone. Whatever God makes He loves

PROVIDENCE

so much that He takes care of it. Ever since the seventh day, God has been taking care of the world. In a way, we can say that all the days and years and centuries since creation are one great seventh day of rest in God's plan. We call God's care for the world His *providence*.

What does God's providence have to do with my life?

For us the most important thing to remember about God's care for the world (His providence) is this: He has a plan for our lives too. Things don't just happen. Life isn't made up of good luck and bad luck. Behind everything that happens in your life is a wise and good plan of God. The world is like a great building that God built according to a plan. Your life is like a temple that He also is building according to a wonderful plan.

When God thinks of you—and He never stops thinking of you—He has in mind a plan of what He wants you to be. He wants you to be His child. But He also has a plan about what He wants you to do for Him when you grow up. He has a plan just for you.

How can I know about God's plan for my life?

You should pray every day that God will show you His plan for your life. Whenever you have to decide what you are going to do, ask God to help you make the right decision.

In order to work out His plan for your life, God gave you the Bible to tell you how to live. It is something like a map. When your family travels, you know where you want to go. Let us say you are planning to go to Washington, D.C. A map shows you where it is. But a map also shows you how to get there. The Bible is like that. It tells you what God wants you to be. It also tells you how to become what God wants you to be. In the Bible you have God's plan for your life. It tells you that God made you, that He saved you, and that He always cares for you.

You want to know God's plan for your life, don't you? Then study His Word, pray to God asking Him to make it clear, and then obey His Word. He promises us that the path will be clear. His word is a lamp to our feet and a light on our path.

Our plans don't always work out. Do God's plans for our lives always work out? Are they always good?

We make plans too, don't we? Sometimes our plans work out— sometimes they don't. Possibly you have planned to go to a birthday party, but you became sick and had to drop your plans. Sometimes your family makes plans for a picnic, only to find that rain comes to spoil those plans. You can never be completely sure about your plans. You might even be called to heaven before your plans work out. That is why you should always say, "If the Lord wills," when you talk about your plans. Sometimes God's plan for you is not your plan. You must learn to be satisfied with God's changes in your plans. He never makes mistakes. His plans are always good. You may not always be able to understand why God does things in a certain way. But you must trust Him still. His plans never fail. And in His plans He is always seeking what is best for you.

Why is it that we sometimes can't understand all of God's plans? Why does He cause things to happen the way they do?

In our lives things sometimes turn out so differently than we had expected. Sometimes there are pleasant surprises, sometimes unpleasant surprises. This is because God doesn't tell us everything He has planned for us. We don't know what will happen tomorrow. Some things we know, because God has revealed them to us. Other things are hidden from us because they are part of the secret will of God.

We see this in the story of Joseph. He went to visit his brothers. That was his plan. But he ended up in a well and later was a slave in Egypt. That was God's plan. God was using those strange events and unpleasant experiences in order to prepare a safe place for Jacob and his family when the time of famine would come. God even took the evil plans of Joseph's brothers and turned them into good. That's why, years later, looking back, Joseph could say:

As for you, ye meant evil against me; but God meant it for good, to bring

to pass, as it is this day, to save much people alive. Genesis 50:20.

This shows God's plan for Joseph's life.

He also has a plan for your life. By reading the Bible and by praying to find out His plan for you, let Him guide you. Work along with His will. Follow where He leads the way.

To help you keep these ideas in your mind, learn the Bible verse in Genesis 50:20.

PRAYER

Heavenly Father, I thank Thee that Thou art a loving Father who never sleeps but always cares for Thy children. I thank and praise Thee for Thy mighty power to control presidents and dictators, thunder and lightning, and also even the smallest things in my life. Teach me to love and trust Thee. Make Thy Word plain to me so that, as I study it, Thy plan for my life may become more clear to me. Help me each day to walk according to Thy plan. In Jesus' name, Amen.

BIBLE VERSE

As for you, ye meant evil against me; but God meant it for good, to bring to pass, as it is this day, to save much people alive. Genesis 50:20

THINKING IN BLACK-ON-WHITE

1. The Bible says God rested after creation. Does this mean that He stopped working? See John 5:17.

2. What is the difference between God's work of creation and God's work of providence?

3. Give some examples of God's providence in our lives.

4. How may you learn about God's plan and purpose for your life? Read Psalm 119:105 and Proverbs 3:5, 6.

5. What lesson about God's providence can you learn from the story of Joseph?

QUESTIONS AND ANSWERS FOR MEMORY WORK

1. **What is the providence of God?**

   The providence of God is His care for the world and His wise plan for our lives.

2. **Can you always understand God's plan for your life?**

   I cannot always understand God's plan for my life, but I can still trust God and believe that He is always seeking my good.

3. **How can you know God's will for your life?**

   I can know God's will for my life by reading and obeying God's Word and by praying that God will lead me.

WHAT DO YOU THINK ABOUT IT?

1. Nancy and her mother made plans to go shopping for a nice dress, which Nancy planned to wear for her birthday party. The day before they were to go shopping, the car broke down and they were unable to go because they lived twelve miles from town. Nancy was terribly disappointed. Her mother tried to explain to Nancy that maybe God didn't want them to go to town. Nancy said, "If God made our car break down, then I hate God." What could Nancy's mother say about that?

2. Jimmy went straight from his class to the street where the boys and girls were sledding. Maple Street was always

blocked off from use by cars so it would be safe for sledding. But today it was not blocked off. Another street was being repaired and cars had to use Maple Street for a few days. The lesson in class had been about God's providence. Jimmy looked at the hill and said, "I'm going sledding anyway. God controls everything. He has a plan for my life. And if I'm going to have an accident, it will happen anyway." What would you say to Jimmy?

3. Tell one or two incidents that show how God's providence has worked in your own life.

YOU ARE A CHILD OF THE KING

Who are you? What are you like? How did God make you? What did God make you for? Why are you here? That's what this lesson is about. It will ask you to think about yourself.

The two most important persons for you to know are God and yourself. In lesson two we learned about God. Listen carefully now as the Bible tells you about yourself.

Have you ever wanted to be a prince or a princess? It must be great to be the child of a king!

The child of a king is called a prince or a princess. Have you ever seen one—a real live one? Of course, you have read about them in books. They live in such grand style. They always seem to have everything. But would you like to see a real live prince or princess right now? I'll tell you how. Go and look in a mirror. Then you will be seeing one.

No, this is not make-believe. We really are children of the King. That is the way God made man. Among all the creatures He made in the world, God gave us the highest place. God is the King of kings. We are His children because He created us. Doesn't this make you feel great!

*We are lower than God, but higher
than everything else God made.*

One of the Psalm writers compares man, God's most wonderful creature, with the other wonderful things God created.
Listen to these words:

When I consider thy heavens, the work of thy fingers,
The moon and the stars, which thou hast ordained;
What is man, that thou art mindful of him?
And the son of man, that thou visitest him?
For thou hast made him but a little lower than God,
And crownest him with glory and honor.
Thou makest him to have dominion over the work of thy
  hands;
Thou hast put all things under his feet.

Psalm 8:3-6

God is, of course, much higher and greater than man. Man
can never become God. But God made man very much like
Himself. Man can think like God, and speak like God, and
work like God. This is true because God is our Father-Creator.
He made us. We are His creatures—His children. In every-
day life children act much like their parents. So we, as children of the King, are able to act much like God. No other
creatures of God have such a high place in God's plan. In the
sight of God we have the highest value. So God was very
displeased when man spoiled things by falling into sin. By
doing this men became like runaway children. But because
God still loved men so much, He sent His eternal Son into the
world to bring men back into His family.

Why did God create man last?

As you know, the most important part of a home is not the
roof or the pets, not the furniture or the plants, but the people
who live there. This is also true of the world—the great home

that God made for man. God first made sky and land and sea. He made plants and animals and birds. He made day and night, summer and winter. But the most important part of this wonderful creation is the people God made.

Everyone knows that people don't move into a home until it is ready. God worked the same way in making the world and man. He waited with creating man until the world was ready for people to live in it. There had to be air to breathe and land on which to live, water to drink and plants to eat. Otherwise man could not live. That is why God waited until the last day of creation, the sixth day, before He created man. He made everything else first so that man could have a good life.

What are we here for?

In God's plan man has a V.I.P. (a very important place) because he is a V.I.P. (a very important person). As the child of the King, man is the prince over creation. Therefore God gave him a very special blessing and a very special task. Notice how the Bible verse for today mentions both our great blessing and our great task.

From the very beginning God told us to rule over the world for Him. He made us to be lords over the animal world and caretakers over the plant world. We were not made to be like princes who sit in their palaces doing nothing. We were given a big job. God gave us work to do. God is the greatest Worker, but He made us to be His co-workers. In this way we can enjoy and make use of the good things God gives us in the world. In this way we can also glorify Him as the Creator.

> *Do you ever wonder what kind of work you will do when you grow up? God gave people different kinds of skills so that people could do different kinds of jobs.*

When we think of the first family that ever lived, we see that they had different kinds of work. God placed Adam in the Garden of Eden to be His gardener. Adam's job was to plant things, and cultivate and harvest them. From the plants that God created, Adam could grow new ones. He could use all the products of creation to make life good and enjoyable.

God gave Eve a task too. As the first mother, she had to bring up her family. She could teach all mothers how to care for children and how to take care of the home.

To both Adam and Eve, and to all parents since that time, God gave the task of training their children and seeing that they get a good education.

Men do different kinds of work because God gave men different kinds of skills. Remember the first two brothers. Cain used the skills God gave him to work as a farmer. Abel used the skills God gave him to work as a herder. Later on the descendants of Cain became herders and musicians and blacksmiths (Genesis 4:20-22).

Work is a blessing given by God.

When your father goes to work to earn a living, whether he works in a factory or on a farm, in an office or in a store, he is really doing the same kind of thing that God told Adam to do. God commands us to work. Work is a good thing. If we are lazy and don't want to work, we are being disobedient to God. Even our Lord Jesus Christ worked as a carpenter. He chose fishermen to be His apostles. Paul was a tent-maker.

Today there are many exciting jobs in the world, many more than in Bible times. We can become builders, doctors, mechanics, farmers, scientists, pilots, ministers, housewives, secretaries, nurses, lawyers, governors, teachers, merchants, or hundreds of other things. For God has given us many different skills. And God lets men discover many wonderful secrets of His great creation. God wants us to use all His good gifts. As His children, we can serve His Kingdom on earth through our work for God and our fellow men.

How should we use our lives?

We are made to be God's workers. But we must work to help people, not to destroy them. Not for war, but for peace. Not to boast about ourselves, but to honor God. We must not work for selfish things, but to serve our fellowmen and to serve God and sing the praises of all creation before our Creator.

You are a prince over the world and a servant of God. That's what God made you for. And that's what it means to be a true child of the King.

PRAYER

Father in heaven, I thank Thee that Thou hast made me Thy servant and a prince over the world. Help me to serve Thy purpose. Teach me to appreciate Thy rich blessings to me. Help me to be Thy faithful servant and do my work well. As I grow up, lead me into work in which I can honor Thee and help my fellowmen. In Jesus' name, Amen.

BIBLE VERSE

And God blessed them: and God said unto them, Be fruitful, and multiply, and replenish the earth, and subdue it; and have dominion over the fish of the sea, and over the birds of the heavens, and over every living thing that moveth upon the earth.

Genesis 1:28

THINKING IN BLACK-ON-WHITE

1. Why may you call yourself the child of a King?
2. Mention some things that show that man is the greatest creature in the world.
3. Why did God make man on the last day of creation?
4. What work did God give man to do?
5. Why is it wrong to hate work?
6. What kinds of work can we do to honor God?

QUESTIONS AND ANSWERS FOR MEMORY WORK

1. **What did God make us to be?**

   God made us to be His children and gave us the highest. place in His creation.

2. **Why did God give us such a very important place?**

God gave us an important place because He wants us to be His workers and rule over the world for Him.

3. **How do we work for God?**

We work for God by using His good gifts to serve our fellowmen and to glorify our Maker.

WHAT DO YOU THINK ABOUT IT?

1. The neighborhood boys were taking a hike through the woods. Down by the creek they caught some turtles and frogs. They decided to have some fun by torturing them. But one boy felt that this would be wrong, and he said so. But the leader of the gang replied, "Our Bible-study book said that we are rulers over the animal world, and so we can do whatever we want to with them." Do you think he was right?

2. Susan loved to do nothing but play all day long. Even though she was already ten years old, she would run away from doing dishes and would put up a big fuss whenever her mother asked her to run an errand. She hated to work and just would not do any work without being forced to do so. What was wrong with Susan's ideas about working?

THE ANGELS ARE GOD'S HELPERS

We have studied about the world of things and people that God made. This week we study about those living beings —the angels—that God made but that we can't see. God created them to serve Him and to serve God's children. What does the Bible teach us about the angels?

All of you like to use your imaginations. When you were younger, you loved to hear and read stories about fairies and elves. Now that you are a little older, you read and listen to stories about ghosts, haunted houses, spooks, and other stories that sometimes cause bad dreams. But really, do you believe that there are ghosts, spooks or fairies? Of course not!

The Bible does teach that there are beings in this world that we can't see. They are invisible because God created them as spirits. In that way they are like God because God is a Spirit. A spirit is a person without a physical body. So there could be one angel or a hundred angels in the room with you right now. Does that idea make you feel good, or does it make you feel a little afraid? Well, we should know more about the angels before we can answer that question.

What kind of beings are the angels?
What do they do?

God made the angels to live with Him in heaven. They sing songs of praise to God and are always ready to do God's work. And God gives them important work to do. Sometimes He sends them down to earth to do His work. They helped God in His work of creation. Many times God sent them as His messengers to tell people about God's plan of salvation. They helped Jesus in His suffering for our sins. Today they still help us to live for God.

Sometimes angels became visible to men.

To do God's work, the angels sometimes showed themselves with bodies that could be seen. Instead of being invisible, they became visible. For example, an angel wrestled with Jacob all night at the Jabbok River. An angel appeared to Joshua as he led Israel into the land of Canaan. An angel appeared to Mary to announce the coming birth of Jesus. A host of angels sang to the shepherds when Jesus was born. An angel helped Peter escape from prison. How many other Bible stories can you remember that tell about angels helping God's people? Today they do the same good work for us even though we cannot see them.

Why are the angels able to help us?

In God's creation everything has a place. God made the angels to serve Him and to help us. The angels are able to help us. They know many more things than we do. They know secrets of the world that are hidden from us. God shows things to angels that He doesn't reveal to us.

Angels can also help us because they are very strong. The angel just touched Jacob's hip and he was a cripple for the rest of his life. And do you remember how the angel of death helped to deliver the Israelites from Egypt at the time of the Passover? Read again the wonderful story of Elisha the prophet who told his servant not to be afraid, even though they were right in the middle of the enemy, because God's angels were all around them (II Kings 6:14-17).

Of course the angels don't know as much as God knows. God knows everything. And they aren't as strong as God. God is all-powerful. But they have great power, and God sends the angels to strengthen you and defend you against sin, the devil, and dangerous enemies.

Angels can help us so well also because they never die. All of us must die. But the angels stay just the same. They never grow old and feeble. So they can keep right on helping people. They helped your grandparents and your parents. They are helping you, and they will help your children some day too. Maybe the same angel who was with Daniel in the lion's den has guarded you from some danger.

Sometimes God sends one angel to do His work. One angel came to Elijah when he was running for his life from Jezebel the wicked queen. But sometimes many angels work together. For example, after Jesus' temptation in the wilderness several angels came to strengthen Him. We don't know how many angels there are. But we can be sure that there is a great army of angels. There are so many angels that no one can count them except God, who is the commander of that great army. Never think that your problem is so big that God can't send angels enough, with wisdom enough, and strength enough, to help you.

Will angels help us in anything we do?

The angels help us only in good things. They try to keep us from evil things. God's angels are holy. They are perfectly good, just as God made them in the beginning. These angels never fell into sin like Adam, and they never disobeyed God in anything. Therefore they are happy when we obey God. And they are displeased when we disobey God, for they are always on God's side.

But remember, the angels are not gods. There is only one God, and He made the angels. They are His servants and helpers. So we may never worship angels or pray to them. We must worship and pray to God alone. When we do this, the angels are happy, because this is what they do too.

But what about the wicked angels?

One last warning! Besides the many good angels who want to help us, there are also many bad angels who want to hurt us. These are Satan—the devil—and his wicked angels who rebelled against God. They are enemies of God. They fight against God's people. They are always bad and will always remain bad. Those wicked angels are always busy trying to make us sin. Whenever they try to make us disobey God, we must say "No" to them, as Jesus did when Satan tempted Him in the wilderness. When we pray to God, He will send good angels to protect us from the bad angels. One day God will send the bad angels to hell forever, and we will live with the good angels in heaven forever, praising and serving God.

We started with this question, Does it make you feel good or does it make you a little afraid to think that there may be angels with you right now? What is your answer?

PRAYER

Dear heavenly Father, I thank Thee for the promises that are given to me in the Bible. Today I thank Thee especially that I am never left alone, but that Thy angels are always ready to help me, to guard me, to keep me from evil. Teach me to love Thee and to serve Thee as the angels do. Teach me to hate evil and love that which is good, as the angels do. Send Thy guardian angels to help me. In Jesus' name, Amen.

BIBLE VERSE

Are they [angels] not all ministering spirits, sent forth to do service for the sake of them that shall inherit salvation?

Hebrews 1:14

THINKING IN BLACK-ON-WHITE

1. What are four ways in which the angels are different from people?
2. God's angels have been busy doing God's work today. Give some examples.
3. How many angels are there?
4. Will the angels help you do *anything?*
5. What does the Bible say about worshiping angels? Read Colossians 2:18 and Revelation 22:8-9.
6. What work do Satan and his angels do? Read I Peter 1:5-8. How can we win out against them? See Matthew 6:13.

QUESTIONS AND ANSWERS FOR MEMORY WORK

1. **Who are the angels?**

   The angels are spirits with great wisdom and power, created by God to serve Him and help us.

2. **What kind of work do the angels do?**

   The angels work as God's servants in creation, providence and salvation, and they watch over our lives every day.

3. **What do the angels help us do?**

   The angels help us worship and serve God, and fight against Satan and sin.

WHAT DO YOU THINK ABOUT IT?

1. Paul's father was a missionary home on vacation. But his family was planning to return to Africa next week. Paul was having dinner at the Stevens', whose son Bob was a friend of Paul. At the table they began to discuss jungle life in Africa. Bob asked whether Paul was afraid to return to such a wild place where he would have to watch out for animals along the trail and shake scorpions out of his shoes. "No," answered Paul, "I believe God's angels work just as hard in Africa to help us as they do in New Jersey." What kind of a boy do you think Paul was?

2. There are some people today who say that an angel once appeared to them. They remember the very place where it happened. Ever since it happened, they go back to that place from time to time to bring their thank offerings and to worship the angel that appeared to them. What do you think about this?

Lesson 7

WHAT WE HAVE LEARNED

A Review Lesson

Before you leave on a trip you always check once more, just before you leave, to see whether you have taken along all the things you will need. After you have gone a hundred miles it is difficult to go back to get them.

In the same way we want to stop before we travel on to the next lessons. Let us see whether we have stored in our minds and in our hearts the important things we should know. We will check up to see whether we have forgotten any of the important things. These are things that we must know if we are going to have a happy journey through life.

Have you packed away the answers to the questions on the next page? If you are not sure, you should go back and read the lessons again and find those answers. There are more questions in this lesson. They also will help you to check up on whether or not you are ready to go on.

Let us see whether we can give you a start to all of the answers with one long sentence.

The Bible came to us from God through many different writers over many centuries to tell us about the great love of God, who created the world according to a good and wise plan, and who also has a plan for our lives, and who made us as His children and to be His workers and to rule over the world, and who made the angels to be His servants and our helpers.

Are you ready for the journey?

1. HOW DID GOD GIVE US THE BIBLE?

2. GOD IS LOVE. WHAT DOES THAT MEAN?

3. HOW DID GOD CREATE THE WORLD?

4. DOES GOD HAVE A PLAN FOR MY LIFE?

5. WHY DID GOD CREATE ME?

6. WHAT ARE ANGELS LIKE?

PRAYER

Father in heaven, I thank Thee for Thy Word, which is my map for my life's journey. I thank Thee for the beautiful world and for giving me work to do here. I thank Thee for the angels who guide and guard me. Most of all I thank Thee for Thy love in sending Jesus Christ. In His name I pray, Amen.

REVIEW QUESTIONS

These questions will help you to review what you have learned.

1. How did God reveal His Word to the Bible authors?
2. How has the Bible come down to us today?
3. Why is the Bible God's "good news" to us?
4. Since God loved us first, how must we answer His love in our daily living?
5. How can we see God's plan in His creation of the world?
6. What can we learn from the fact that God rested on the seventh day after six days of creation?
7. What is the providence of God?
8. How can we know God's plan for our lives?
9. What place did God give us in His creation?
10. How must we use our lives?
11. What are angels?
12. What work has God given the angels to do?

WE ARE GREAT SINNERS

This lesson is about the worst thing that ever happened in the world. It happened long ago, when man fell into sin. The result of it is still with us today. Sin is so bad because it spoils the good things God made; it even spoiled man. In lesson four we saw what we were like when God made us. In this lesson we shall look at ourselves as we are now. All of us are sinners. No one likes to hear this, but it is true, because the Bible says so and we can feel it. It is important to feel our sins, because otherwise we will not seek the Savior. Then we will miss the best thing in the world.

Have you ever been perfect for a month, or a week, or even for a whole day? Anyone who says "Yes" is not telling the truth. Do you ever wonder why it is that on some days you just can't seem to do anything right? Why do you sometimes become terribly naughty? You don't really want to talk back to people or steal things or lie, do you? And yet you do it. Why? And why do even grown-ups sin? Have you ever asked yourself where sickness and pain, sorrow and sadness come from?

The answer to all these questions lies in one little word with three letters—S I N. Sin is a disease. All of us have this disease. All of us need the healing from sin that only Jesus can give.

How did sin get started?

Sometimes we say to ourselves, "If only things had stayed the way God made them!" Then everybody would be happy. Then we wouldn't cry. Then there wouldn't be any terrible wars. But this is one of those big "ifs." For we know that sin did enter the world when Adam disobeyed God. This spoiled everything. Then God became angry with man, and He had a right to be angry.

The Bible tells us in Genesis 3 how sin got started. Then the biggest change in the world happened. It happened when man listened to Satan and turned away from God.

What did we do to make ourselves sinners?

We all know that laws are made to help us live good lives. When we obey the laws at home and at school and in our cities, then things go well. But when we disobey the laws, then we must look for trouble.

This is the way it was in Paradise too. God gave Adam His good laws. He could eat of all the trees in the garden, except the Tree of Knowledge. If Adam had obeyed God's commandment, everything would have remained wonderful. But he disobeyed. He listened to Satan instead of to God. From that time on Adam became a sinner. Because he is our father and represented us, we all became his disobedient children. We see sin at work in Adam and Eve's children when Cain killed Abel. In the days of Noah sin became so great that God had to destroy the world with a flood.

By sinning, we and all men rebelled against God's rule over us. In the beginning of the world we were on God's side. God warned us about the results of sin. But by disobeying God we went over to Satan's side. Only Jesus can bring us back to God's side.

Are all men sinners?

There is an old New England alphabet book that teaches the letter *A* with this little verse: "In Adam's fall we sinned All." Only one Man ever lived on earth who was not a sinner, and you know who He is.

Many people don't like the Bible because it tells us the truth about ourselves. They don't like to hear about their sins. It hurts their pride. They want to think that they are good and don't need a Savior. But Paul tells us in Romans 3:23: "For all have sinned, and all fall short of the glory of God." Our Bible text also teaches us that, "If we say that we have no sin, we deceive ourselves, and the truth is not in us" (I John 1:8).

Can we save ourselves from our sin?

Sin means that we are in trouble—in trouble with God, in trouble with other people, in trouble with ourselves. You have all been in trouble, haven't you? Perhaps you have locked yourself in the bathroom. Or perhaps you have been in a fight with a neighborhood gang. What do you do when you are in trouble? You call for help, don't you?

That is the way it is with sin too. Sin means that we are in such deep trouble that we can't help ourselves. So we call for help. God answers our call. He sent Jesus to help us out of our troubles of sin.

But some people think they can help themselves. Remember the Pharisee who went to the temple to pray. He thought he didn't need God's help. He was proud of himself. He boasted to God about his own goodness. He didn't realize that he was in trouble and that he was a helpless sinner.

There was another man who prayed in the temple at the same time. The publican knew he was a great sinner. So he was honest and humble in his prayer. Listen to his words: "God, be thou merciful to me a sinner" (Luke 18:13).

Jesus tells us that the Pharisee didn't really pray at all. Only the publican went home with God's blessing upon him. For he trusted in God to help him out of his sins.

In what ways do we sin?

In school we often pray these words from the Lord's Prayer: "Forgive us our debts as we forgive our debtors." In our evening prayers we sometimes say without thinking, "Lord, forgive all my sins." But we must mean what we say. For we sin in more ways than we can count.

Let's think of some ways. We sin in the wrong things we *do:* for example, when we steal someone's ball. We also sin in the wrong things we *say:* for example, when we say mean things about some friend. We sin even in the wrong things we *think:* Jesus teaches us in the Sermon on the Mount that hating a person in our hearts is like sowing seeds of murder. God gave us the Ten Commandments to remind us of our many sins, so that we would ask Him to forgive us.

This may surprise you, but we can also sin by doing nothing. If we have a chance to do a good deed but don't do it, we are sinning. If we have a chance to say a good word, like correcting people who are swearing, but don't do it, we are sinning. If we have bad thoughts in our minds, but don't try to get rid of them, we are

sinning. If we don't tell people about Jesus, we are sinning.

You see, we must start with our own sins. If we do, we will find so many sins to confess to God that we won't have much time to talk about other people's sins.

We need God's help to get rid of our sins. We are helpless. That is why God gave us a mighty Savior. Next week we will learn more about Him.

PRAYER

O God, Thou art strong and holy. I am weak and sinful. I confess that I have sinned against Thee in my deeds and words and thoughts. Often I have failed to do what I should have done. I am truly sorry for all my sins. Please forgive me, for Jesus' sake, Amen.

BIBLE VERSE

If we say that we have no sin, we deceive ourselves, and the truth is not in us.   I John 1:8

THINKING IN BLACK-ON-WHITE

1. Is there anyone other than Jesus who has ever lived a perfect life? Look up Romans 3:10-12.
2. Describe how life before man's fall into sin was different from now.
3. Explain why we call sin disobedience to God.
4. Explain why we call sin rebellion against God.
5. Why do some people hate it when the Bible tells them they are sinners?
6. Why can't we save ourselves from our sins? See John 8:34.

7. Mention some different ways in which we sin in our lives.
8. Why do we need a mighty Savior? Read Romans 7:18-25. Why did Paul need a mighty Savior? Are you like Paul in this?

QUESTIONS AND ANSWERS FOR MEMORY WORK

1. **What is sin?**
   Sin is disobedience and rebellion against God.

2. **Are all men sinners?**
   Yes, all men are sinners and need Jesus as their Savior.

3. **In what ways do you sin against God?**
   I sin against God in my evil deeds and words and thoughts, and in the good things that I fail to do.

4. **Why do you need a mighty Savior?**
   I need a mighty Savior because sin has made me so weak and helpless that I cannot do God's will in my own strength.

WHAT DO YOU THINK ABOUT IT?

1. Tim was reading a book about New York City with his brother John. After they had read for a while Tim said, "I'm glad we don't live there because there are awful sinners in those big cities—gangsters, and bank robbers, and bad people like that. We don't have sinners in our little village." If you were John, what would you say about this?

2. There was one thing Karen didn't like about going to church. That was the reading of the Ten Commandments. Every Sunday her minister read them. She didn't like this because every time he read the words, "Thou shalt not steal," it reminded her of the time she stole a pen from the desk across the aisle in school. It bothered her. She never told her mother. She hid the pen deep under some clothes in her drawer. But she hated to be reminded every Sunday of what she had done. Do you think Karen was right about not liking the Ten Commandments? What should she do about it?

GOD PROMISES VICTORY OVER SIN

Of course you know the song "Jesus Loves Me." One line in that song says, "We are weak, but He is strong." Last week we saw how man lost the battle against Satan. Now we are weak and helpless. But God did something about it. He sent His Son into the world as the mighty Conqueror of Satan and as our Savior from sin. This great story of victory did not start on the first Christmas day when Jesus was born. It started way back in the Old Testament. Let's follow this story and see how God prepared the world for the coming of Christ.

Why did Jesus have to fight for us?

In Paradise man lost the first battle against Satan. Was the war all over then? No, the war between God and His followers and Satan and his followers went on for many, many years, until finally Jesus came to win the victory on the cross.

Only Jesus could win this war for us. For by disobeying God we became slaves of Satan. By rebelling against God we went over to Satan's side. By our sins we became so weak and helpless that we couldn't fight back. It took a mighty Savior to fight for us, to win us back to God's side, and to free us from Satan's slavery.

*The Old Testament announced the
coming of the King.*

In the olden days kings ruled with great power. That is
why Jesus came as a King. When a king comes to visit, there
is much preparation. His coming is usually announced long
before he arrives. Messengers and trumpeters prepare the way
for him. Then when the king finally comes, the people stand
ready to greet him.

This is the way it happened with King Jesus too. It started
hundreds of years before His birth. God promised the coming
of the King to the men of the Old Testament. The prophets
announced that it was getting closer. In this way God prepared the world before sending His Son. Many were surprised
and even disappointed at His coming because they didn't listen
carefully to God's announcements. This mighty King came as
the Conqueror of sin. But that was not the kind of king they
wanted, and so they wouldn't join His side.

*How does the Old Testament point
forward to the coming King?*

Right after Adam fell into the hands of Satan, God came
to rescue him. If God had left man alone, we could never have
won the fight against sin. Then there would be no hope of
victory. But God was good to us—He promised a great Savior.
God promised that there would be a big battle. Satan's helpers
would be able to hurt us. But in the end Satan would be defeated by Christ. That is what this week's Bible Text is about.
Read it in Genesis 3:15.

But God didn't tell the whole story all at once. Little by
little He made bigger and bigger promises.

God told Abraham that, through him and his descendants,
He would give a blessing to the whole world. Read Genesis
12:2, 3.

Even the weakling prophet Balaam was speaking for God when he said that "there shall come forth a star out of Jacob, and a sceptre shall arise out of Israel." In those days a star stood for the birth of a king and the sceptre was the sign of power. This, too, pointed toward the coming Christ. Read Numbers 24:17.

Upon his deathbed old father Jacob made this prophecy: "The sceptre shall not depart from Judah, nor the ruler's staff from between his feet, until Shiloh come; and unto him shall the obedience of the peoples be." God promised here that the coming King would be born from the house of Judah.

We get our clearest picture of the coming King from the life of King David. He was God's chosen ruler. He fought the battles of the Lord. He showed the power of God in winning victories and in freeing God's people from their enemies. Remember his fight with the giant Goliath? This was not just a battle between two soldiers, or between two nations. This was a battle between the armies of God and the armies of Satan. Goliath boasted of the strength of his idols. But David fought for the honor of God. God gave the victory to David. This is a picture of Christ's victory over evil for us. For King Jesus is the great Son of King David. Read I Samuel 17:45-47.

Let's take one more example. The prophet Isaiah also promised the coming of the Mighty God who would sit upon the throne of David. King Jesus would build a kingdom that would last forever. Read Isaiah 9:6, 7.

Did all the people welcome King Jesus?

You would expect everyone to welcome this King. But remember what happened when Jesus rode into Jerusalem as King on Palm Sunday? Many people turned against Him. Why? Because all they wanted was a king to fight against the Roman soldiers. They were not interested in One who would conquer sin and Satan and hell for them. They wanted only a man with a sword, not a Man with God's Word. They thought only of a grand throne of ivory in a palace of gold. Jesus gained the throne by dying on a wooden cross on a hill. There He won the victory. But many people didn't believe that this was the kind of King they needed.

The final announcement.

Read Luke 1:31-33. This was God's final announcement. It was brought by the angel Gabriel. It was given to the mother of the King a short time before His birth. Read slowly and carefully the wonderful words about King Jesus.

He is both the great Son of David and the Son of God. That explains why, when Jesus finally came, John the Baptist called Him "the Lamb of God that taketh away the sin of the world." Jesus is so great, John said, that no man is worthy to stoop down and untie His shoestrings. Read John 1:27-29.

He is the mighty Conqueror who saves us from our sins. He is the great King who brought the Kingdom of Heaven down to earth. He won the victory for us. Now He wants us to be on His side in the battle against sin. He wants us to be strong soldiers of the cross and fight the good fight.

PRAYER

Jesus, my Lord and King, I thank Thee for Thy great victory over sin and Satan and hell. I am weak, but Thou art strong. I thank Thee for Thy wonderful power to save me from trouble. Keep me always on Thy side in the battle against evil. Help me to fight the good fight, for Thy name's sake, Amen.

BIBLE VERSE

I will put enmity between thee and the woman, and between thy seed and her seed: he shall bruise thy head, and thou shalt bruise his heel.

Genesis 3:15

THINKING IN BLACK-ON-WHITE

1. Why did God give the Old Testament promises of the coming of Jesus little by little instead of all at once?

2. In what ways is Jesus like a king?

3. Think of some ways in which King David was like King Jesus.

4. How did Jesus win the victory for us?

5. Why did some people turn away from Jesus the King? Read John 6:60-67.

6. How do we show that we are on Jesus' side? See II Timothy 4:7.

QUESTIONS AND ANSWERS FOR MEMORY WORK

1. **How did God prepare the world for the coming of the promised Savior?**

   God prepared the way for the promised Savior by announcing His coming in the Old Testament.

2. **How does the Old Testament announce the coming of Jesus the King?**

In the Old Testament God promised that a star would appear, announcing the birth of a wonderful King, who would be both Mighty God and Son of David, and bring salvation to the world.

3. **What kind of a King is Jesus?**

King Jesus is the mighty Conqueror who won the victory on the cross and is able to save us from our sins.

4. **What does King Jesus want you to do?**

King Jesus wants me to be on God's side in the battle against sin and to fight the good fight of faith.

WHAT DO YOU THINK ABOUT IT?

1. "Well," said Father as he reached for the Bible Story Book after dinner, "shall we read a story from the Old Testament or from the New Testament?" Mary was the first to answer. "From the New Testament," she said, "because I want a story about Jesus, and there is nothing about Jesus in the Old Testament." Was Mary right?

2. Today there are still many people who turn away from King Jesus. Sometimes they call Him a weakling, because if He were really strong and mighty, He would not have let men kill Him on the cross. How would you try to show these people that Jesus' death on the cross proves His great power and His wonderful victory?

FROM A CASTLE TO A CRADLE

Last week we saw Jesus as the mighty King whom God promised in the Old Testament. Now we shall see how this promise came true. If the heavenly King had stayed in His palace of glory, He could not help us. That is why He came to earth. But if He had come to earth only as the Son of God, He would stand high above us and would not come down to our level. That is why He became man like us. The great King of Heaven stooped down and became a child and then a boy and then a man, like us, so that He could be our Savior.

One of the most horrible people of history was King Herod the Great. He was a terribly selfish and jealous person. Have you ever thought what it would be like to be a member of his court? Well, it wasn't very safe. He ordered many of his relatives to be killed—his wife, his sons, and others. He always feared that people were plotting against him. It was really safer to be his pet than his child. With his secret agents moving all around the country, people's lives were always in danger.

What Herod feared most was the rise of a new king of the Jews. That is why he became so upset when the Wisemen came and asked, "Where is he that is born King of the Jews, for we have seen his star in the east and are come to worship him." Herod tried to hide his fear and hatred. He asked the Wisemen to find the Child and then tell him about it, so he could worship the Child too. But you know the rest of the

story, how Herod's soldiers murdered the children of Bethlehem trying to get rid of this newborn King.

What kind of King is this Child?

Herod was wrong about many things, and he was all wrong about this King. Jesus came into the world, not to fight with chariots and swords, as Herod feared. He did not come to overthrow kings and make war against nations. King Jesus came as God's Servant, sent into the world to serve us by saving us from our sins, and to win us over to His side by showing us the great love of God.

Even the Wisemen were partly wrong about Jesus. They came looking for Him in Jerusalem, the capital city. They thought He would be born like a prince in a palace. They expected to take part in a grand celebration of His birth.

But Jesus is not this kind of King. He is like a king who steps down from his royal throne and becomes a servant, helping those who need his help. Jesus is a humble King, born into the family of a plain village maiden and a simple carpenter, born in a backyard stable in the little town of Bethlehem.

You see, God's ideas about sending His Son into the world were far different from some men's ideas. Remember how you sing about it at Christmas time?

Who came down from heaven to earth?
Jesus Christ my Savior.
Born a Child of lowly birth;
Jesus Christ my Savior.

What glory did Jesus have before
He came to earth?

Jesus was not a king like many other kings. He was the King over all kings. He was the Ruler of heaven and earth. He was the Son of God. All the glories of heaven were His to enjoy and use. He had helped the Father in the work of creation. He had sent angels as messengers to announce His own coming. He had strengthened His people in their battles against the enemy.

We can't even imagine what a wonderful life Jesus had before He was born in Bethlehem. Only when we get to heaven will we begin to understand it.

You see, Jesus didn't start living on the first Christmas Day. He was living long before that. Jesus was alive long before the giant redwood trees in California began growing, even long before Adam, the first man, was created. He is the Son of God, and so we know that He was *always* living.

All of us began living when we were born. But Jesus had no beginning. He is eternal. All the power and riches and glory were His forever as the Son of God.

What happened that first Christmas
Day? God became man. What did
this mean for Jesus?

All of us have a birthday and a place of birth. This was true of Jesus too. Jesus the Savior was born in Bethlehem more than 1900 years ago. As the Son of God, He became like us in everything, except sin. After Christmas Day in Bethlehem Jesus was both God and man.

This is very hard to understand, isn't it? There is no other person like Jesus. No one can really understand what it means that God became man. It is a great mystery. But still we believe this truth, because this is what the Bible tells us.

Man is God's highest creature. But he is still far below God. So Jesus had to stoop way down to become like us. He had to humble Himself by laying aside His heavenly robes and His crown. If Jesus had been born in the beautiful court of Herod in Jerusalem, or even if He had been born in the most wonderful palace in all the world, this would still mean that Jesus had humbled Himself. For there is no castle on earth glorious enough to receive the heavenly King.

But now remember what really happened. There was no place for Him in the inn, no room in a house. He was born in a cattle shed. No servants, no noblemen were there. Only Joseph and Mary were there. All this added to Jesus' humiliation. He stepped down from the richest throne in heaven to the poorest shelter on earth. Yet He did it willingly. He did it for us.

Into what kind of world did Jesus come? Why did He come?

Many years ago there was a snowbound village in Alaska. A terrible disease struck the people. There was no doctor, and medicine was many miles away. Unless a doctor came with medicine, everyone would die. So some brave men fought their way through the storm, bringing a doctor and medicine. In this way the village was saved.

What Jesus did was something like that. We all had the sickness of sin. We could not help each other because we were all sick. The only hope was from outside the world. God sent His Son into the world to cure us of the terrible power of sin.

To do this, Jesus had to go into a strange world—a world very different from His heavenly home. For heaven is pure and holy. He left this home to enter a world of sin and evil.

He left the pearly gates and the streets of gold to be born in a feeding box, on a bunch of straw, wrapped in swaddling clothes, with cattle standing close by.

This was part of God's wonderful plan of salvation for your life. Jesus was happy to humble Himself and do it for you. Think of this when you learn the Bible Text, and be thankful.

Out of the ivory palaces, into a world of woe,
Only His great redeeming love made my Savior go.

PRAYER

Dear Lord Jesus, I thank Thee for coming down into our world. I am sorry there was no room for Thee in the inn. Help me to make room for Thee in my heart. I thank Thee for Thy great humility in coming down where I am to save me. Help me to be humble too. Thou hast done so much for me. Help me to live for Thee. In Thy name I ask it, Amen.

BIBLE VERSE

Ye know the grace of our Lord Jesus Christ, that, though he was rich, yet for your sakes he became poor, that ye through his poverty might become rich. II Corinthians 8:9

THINKING IN BLACK-ON-WHITE

1. How is Jesus, the heavenly King, different from earthly kings?

2. Describe some of the glorious and wonderful things Jesus had to leave behind when He came from heaven to earth.

3. What does it mean that Jesus is eternal? Read John 8: 56-59.

4. Mention some things about Jesus' birth in Bethlehem that show that this was a very humble beginning for our Savior.

5. Read Philippians 2:5-7. Paul tells us there that we in our

lives should show the same humble spirit that Jesus showed. How can we show in our lives that we are humble?

QUESTIONS AND ANSWERS FOR MEMORY WORK

1. **What does the Bible teach us about the birth of Jesus?**
   The Bible teaches us that Jesus the eternal Son of God became the Son of Man by being born in Bethlehem.

2. **What was so humble about the birth of Jesus?**
   As the heavenly King, Jesus humbled Himself and became a Servant, laying aside His power and glory to become our Savior.

3. **What does Jesus' humble birth mean for us?**
   We must be thankful for Jesus' humble birth, give our lives to Him, and then serve God and man in a humble spirit.

WHAT DO YOU THINK ABOUT IT?

1. Linda and Beckie were drawing pictures about the birth of Jesus in Bethlehem. Beckie leaned over and looked at Linda's picture. "What is that bright circle around the Baby's head?" she asked. "Why, that's one of those halos," answered Linda. "You know—a ring of light that angels and kings had around their heads in old paintings." Do you think Jesus really had a halo around His head? Give some reasons for your answer.

2. Jack's parents said he could invite a boy friend to go along on a camping trip. Whom would he ask? Jack wanted to take Carl along. Carl went camping often. His parents always gave him a lot of spending money to take along. Carl had a very expensive lantern and nice clothes. Jack always felt proud to be with Carl. But Jack's dad said, "What about Henry?" Henry never got a chance to go camping because his father was too sick to work, and so they didn't have money to go on vacation. But to Jack it seemed that Henry didn't have much to be proud of. If you were Jack, how would you solve this problem?

THE KING LIVES LIKE A SERVANT

Sallman's **Head of Christ** used by permission of the copyright owners, Krieble & Bates.

When we think of Jesus' humble birth in Bethlehem, as we did last week, we sometimes say, "Poor Jesus!" But Jesus doesn't need our pity, and He doesn't want it. He only wants us to believe that, though He was a Child, He was also our King. When He grew up He kept on being the Servant of God, even though He was also our Master. He tells us the theme of His whole life when He said that He came "not to be served, but to serve" (Matthew 20:28 RVS). He didn't live for Himself, but for His people. As the great Servant of God He gave Himself for us and set an example for our lives.

In olden days in Russia a king was called a Czar (pronounced "zar"). There was once a Czar named Nicholas II. Like many rulers he was rich and lived in a palace. But most of his people were very poor. Some kings never bothered much about how their people lived. But Czar Nicholas II loved his people. He wanted to know what their life was like so he could help them. Sometimes he would leave the palace dressed like a poor man and walk down the streets of the city. His people didn't know that he was the Czar because he looked like them. He would stop and talk to his people about their troubles. In this way he tried to find ways to use his power as Czar to do some good.

Why did Jesus leave His palace in heaven to live like people on earth?

Jesus was something like Czar Nicholas II, except that Jesus lived like that all the time while He was on earth, not just once in a while. He was a greater King than the Russian Czar. Still He lived among men as God's humble and willing Servant.

Look at the life of Jesus. He met all kinds of people. He lived like the other people of His times. He was friendly to all, except those who went against Him. John the Baptist preached and baptized at the Jordan River. He waited for people to come to him. But Jesus did more. He visited them wherever they were. So in the Bible we find Jesus in the temple and in the synagogues, at the marketplaces, along the roads, down by the boat docks, on the farms, at wedding feasts and banquets—almost everywhere.

Wherever Jesus went He talked to people, because He had a message to tell. At twelve years of age He talked to ministers in the temple. Later He talked with farmers and carpenters and shepherds and fishermen and mothers and teachers and slaves and tax-collectors — all kinds of people. He walked with them and talked with them because these were the kinds of people He came to

save. He tried to find out their needs so that He could help them.

> *How can a king be a good servant,*
> *unless he lives with his people?*

Some people think that we as Christians should move away from all other people in order to live a good life. They say we should live in a world all by ourselves. They say we should build a city with high walls to keep all other people out, or that we should settle on some deserted South Sea island.

But Jesus didn't live that way. He didn't act as if He were too good to be with sinful people, even though He was perfect. How could He be a Servant to sinners unless He lived close to them? That is why we see Jesus going everywhere doing good, teaching and preaching and healing. He visited in people's homes. He worshiped in their churches. He traveled with them. He helped them with their work. He joined them in their meals.

> *How did King Jesus show that He was*
> *God's humble Servant?*

There was nothing proud about Jesus. He was our humble and friendly Master. We can really sing, "What a Friend we have in Jesus."

Do you remember the temptations in the wilderness? For forty days Jesus humbled Himself before God, going without food or drink. Then Satan came. He tried to make Jesus use His great power to satisfy Himself, like turning stones into bread to satisfy His hunger and jumping from the steeple of the temple so people would recognize Him. But Jesus said, "No!" For He did not come into the world to use His powers to help Himself, but to help others.

One day some mothers came to bring their children to Jesus. The disciples tried to chase these people away. They thought Jesus was too important to be bothered with such little things.

But Jesus wants to be a Servant even for little children. Therefore He said, "Suffer the little children, and forbid them not, to come unto me: for to such belongeth the kingdom of heaven" (Matthew 19:14).

Do you remember when Jesus fed the five thousand people? They all thought this miracle was so wonderful that they decided to make Jesus their King that very hour. But Jesus didn't want the glories of an earthly empire. He knew He must be God's humble Servant in order to save sinners. So He turned down this honor. He was using His mighty miracles, not to win the praise of men, but to show that He was the Savior and to reveal the great love of God to men.

Even the twelve disciples forgot that Jesus came to be a humble Servant. That is why they sometimes asked Him to call down lightning upon His enemies, and to use His power to destroy wicked men, and to set up His kingdom by a war. Then Jesus had to remind them that this is not the way God's Servant was to save us.

> *Do you remember the best example Jesus*
> *gave us of humble service to others?*

Read John 13:1-17. Here Jesus acts out the story of His life. It happened in the Upper Room. The Master was celebrating the last Passover with His disciples. In those days

people wore sandals. On dirt roads their feet would become very dusty. Before going to the table to eat, a servant would usually wash the feet of the guests. But there was no servant here. Who would do the job? Who would be willing to wash dusty feet?

Jesus looked up and down the table, but no one got up. No one wanted to be a humble, lowly servant. At last, to teach them and us a lesson, Jesus arose from the table. He took a basin of water and a towel and began washing feet.

The disciples, especially Peter, complained loudly. This was no job for their Master! But then Jesus told them a secret. Washing their feet was a sign of how Jesus washes our whole life clean from sin. So Jesus must be a Servant for all of us, otherwise we do not belong to Him.

Since Jesus our Master became our Servant, we must also become servants of each other. This was Jesus' lesson. He is our great Example. From this we must learn that, in God's sight, the greatest people in the world are those who become humble servants of Christ by unselfishly helping other people.

PRAYER

Lord Jesus, my Savior and my Master, I thank Thee for living in my kind of world, for living among my kind of people, and for living with my kind of problems. Now I am sure that Thou knowest all about me. As God's Servant Thou hast saved me. As my Servant Thou hast given me an example. Help me to follow Thy example and be a humble servant to others. In Thy name I pray, Amen.

BIBLE VERSE

I am in the midst of you as he that serveth.

Luke 22:27

THINKING IN BLACK-ON-WHITE

1. Why did Jesus visit many different places and speak with many different kinds of people during His life?
2. What do you think about the idea that Christians should separate themselves from the world?
3. How do the miracles of Jesus reveal Him as the mighty King?
4. How do the miracles of Jesus reveal Him as the humble Servant?
5. Why would it have been wrong for Jesus to obey Satan when He was tempted in the wilderness (Matthew 4:1-11)?
6. When Jesus washed the disciples' feet, what great truth did He teach us about what He does when He saves us?
7. How can we follow Jesus' example of washing the disciples' feet?

QUESTIONS AND ANSWERS FOR MEMORY WORK

1. **What does the Bible teach us about the life of Christ?**
   The Bible teaches us that during His whole life Christ humbled Himself as the Servant of God and, except for sin, became like us in all things.

2. **How did Jesus show in His life that He was a humble Servant?**
   Jesus showed us that He was a humble Servant by using His mighty power, not to honor and glorify Himself, but to save and help His people.

3. **What example of humble service did Jesus give us?**
   Jesus our Master gave us an example when He washed His disciples' feet, and so we as His disciples ought to serve each other in humility and love.

WHAT DO YOU THINK ABOUT IT?

1. When Grace found out that the Van Stoken family around the corner never went to church and didn't read the Bible

or pray, she was very upset about it. She didn't talk to anyone about it. But she thought about it quite a bit. Finally she decided what she would do. Since they were not Christians, she would have nothing to do with them. She wouldn't play with Carol Van Stoken. She wouldn't speak to any of them. She would act as if they were not even around. Is this the way Jesus treated people? What would Jesus want Grace to do?

2. It was a terribly hard decision for Sam to make! Roy and his father had invited Sam to join them on a three-day fishing trip to Minnesota, from Thursday until Saturday. Sam could just imagine the fun they would have. But then there was that other thing. Sam's parents had planned a quick trip up to Wisconsin, Friday and Saturday, to visit Sam's grandmother. She was very ill and was not expected to live very long. Grandmother Bennet had made a special request for Sam to see her this time. Now Sam sat there thinking. Which was more important: his fun or his grandmother's request? Which do you think was more important?

CHRIST OUR WONDERFUL SAVIOR

We met Christ presented in the Old Testament as the great King whom God promised to His people. In His birth at Bethlehem Christ was also great, even though His greatness lay hidden in swaddling clothes. During His life on earth Christ was great, even though He lived like a Servant. But Christ showed His greatness most wonderfully in His suffering and death. The day of the cross was His greatest day, and ours too. For Christ's death was not a mistake in God's plans or a defeat at the hands of His enemies. The cross stands for victory.

When did Christ's suffering begin?
How long did His sufferings last?

All of us were born to live. But with Christ it was different. He was born in order to die. He came into the world knowing that He would give His life as a sacrifice for us.

In your thoughts go with me for a minute to Bethlehem. Along the road on the north side of this village is a signpost that reads, "Jerusalem, 7 miles." This is a very short road, isn't it? That road is a picture of Christ's life. Christ came to earth to walk that road. He started that road in Bethlehem. The end of that road was Calvary, where Christ died. Along the way He went many other places. But in the end He came back to that road. From the very start He could see the cross standing ahead of Him, and step by step He moved closer to it.

While Christ walked that road from birth to death, He was very great. He knew that He was the Lamb of God who came to take away the sins of the world by laying down His life. That is the way it had to be. And that is the way Christ wanted it to be.

Many artists have tried to paint pictures of the life of Christ. Long ago a certain artist made a painting of the boy Jesus in Joseph's carpenter shop. The sunlight was streaming in from a window. It shone upon the boy Jesus as He was carrying a long board. The shadow of that board fell upon the wall in the form of a cross. The artist was trying to show that Jesus was carrying the thought of the cross with Him His whole life long. What a terrible future for Jesus! Yet He looked ahead willingly and bravely. What a wonderful Savior we have!

Why did Jesus go through with it and not try to get out of it?

Toward the end of His life Christ's sufferings became worse and worse. There was no help for Him. For He was the only One who could suffer and die for us. No one else could do it for Him.

If it was so awful, why did Jesus go through with it? He kept going because He knew that His Father in heaven wanted Him to do it. This was God's plan for our salvation. That is why He never tried to get out of it. When the time came for Him to die, He went straight up to Jerusalem. He even set the time for His own death. It could not happen until He was ready. That is why He often said, "My hour is not yet come." But when the hour came, He willingly laid down His life for us.

It was not easy for Jesus to die. For death is an enemy. Death came into the world because of sin. But Jesus came to conquer sin. To do that He had to die. This shows how much He loved us.

At last it was Thursday night. The next day would be Good Friday, when Jesus would die. Jesus went into the Garden of Gethsemane. He could already feel the cross coming upon Him. As He thought about it, He suffered terribly because His

death would be worse than any other person's death. Dying for the sins of His people, He would die many deaths in one. His soul was filled with sorrow. His shoulders were bent low. He kneeled upon the ground; His sweat was like great drops of blood. It was almost too much even for Him to bear.

Then He prayed, "Father, if it be possible, take this bitter cup of suffering from Me. But still I want to do Thy will, not My will." When Jesus had prayed, He was ready to go all the way to the cross. Nothing could stop Him now.

Who captured Jesus? Was it Judas and his followers? Or was it the leaders of the Jews? None of these really captured Jesus. Jesus gave Himself up!

As Jesus was leaving the garden, Judas came up with his soldiers. Did Jesus try to run away? No, He faced them like a king. Jesus knew about Judas' wicked plan. Yet He let Judas kiss Him. He asked the troops, "Whom are you looking for?" "For Jesus," they answered. When He answered, "I am He," they were so shocked that they were knocked over backwards at the mighty word of Jesus.

Peter wanted to fight for his Lord. So he struck off the ear of the high priest's servant. But Jesus said to Peter, "Put away your sword." He even took time to heal the ear of the high priest's servant. Was Jesus a poor, helpless victim? No, He was in full command of the whole situation.

Jesus could have asked His Father to send an army of angels to defend Him. But He didn't because He had made up His mind to go to the cross for us. This was the only way in which we could be saved from our sins. So He surrendered to the soldiers. They could not arrest Him unless He let them do it, for He was greater than all those soldiers. But He let them capture Him, so that He could die for us.

> *Who sent Jesus to the cross? Was it Pilate? Or the Jews? None of these, for it was really God who so loved the world that He sent Jesus to the cross.*

Quickly they held a trial for Jesus. The witnesses told a lot of lies about Him. No one proved that He was guilty, but still they cried, "Crucify Him!"

There was only one great person at the trial, and that was Jesus. Pilate was a coward. The people were evil. Jesus stood there calm, and perfectly good.

Who really pronounced the judgment over Jesus? Was it Pilate who said, "Take Him away"? Or was it the Jews who screamed, "Let Him be crucified"? No, none of these *sentenced* Jesus. This was God's verdict, "Thou, my Son, art the greatest sinner of all. For I have laid upon Thee the sins of all my people. Thou shalt die for them." So Jesus traveled the last steps that led Him to the cross.

The last stop was the cross. He was so weak that He could hardly make it. Yet He kept on going forward, because He wanted the cross. So great was His love for us! Christ was great in His life. He was also great in His death.

The soldiers nailed Him to the cross. Still He prayed for those who were crucifying Him. He remembered to take care of His mother. Even when the crowd made fun of Him, He returned good for evil.

Who is this Man? He is your Savior, your King. No one but Jesus could do all that for you.

O Christ, how great Thou art!

Listen to the captain standing near the cross who, looking up, said, "Truly this was the Son of God!"

PRAYER

Father in heaven, I thank Thee for sending Thy Son into the world to be my Savior. Lord Jesus, I thank Thee for Thy greatness in suffering and dying for my sins. Holy Spirit, I thank Thee for making me a child of God. Amen.

BIBLE VERSE

He humbled himself, becoming obedient even unto death, yea, the death of the cross. Philippians 2:8

THINKING IN BLACK-ON-WHITE

1. When did Jesus begin to suffer in His life?
2. When did His suffering become greatest?
3. What was the great goal in Jesus' life that He always kept in mind? Read Luke 2:49 and John 4:34.
4. What made Jesus want to go all the way to the cross and not try to get out of it? See Matthew 20:28.
5. How did Jesus show His greatness over Judas and the soldiers who came to arrest Him?
6. How did Jesus show His greatness even while dying on the cross?

QUESTIONS AND ANSWERS FOR MEMORY WORK

1. **What does the suffering and death of Christ teach us?**
   The suffering and death of Christ teaches us what a great and wonderful Savior we have.

2. **What gave Jesus the strength to carry out God's plan of salvation?**

Jesus was strengthened to carry out God's plan of salvation by the knowledge that He was doing His Father's will.

3. **How did Jesus die?**

Jesus died on a cross, freely giving His life for us.

WHAT DO YOU THINK ABOUT IT?

1. On the way to the cross some women were standing along the road watching Jesus go. They were so filled with pity, as they saw the shame and suffering of Jesus, that they began to cry. Jesus turned to them and said, "Don't cry for Me." Why didn't Jesus want them to shed tears over Him? What did Jesus want instead of pity? How does this show His greatness?

2. Joey and Sheryl were reading a Bible story book before going to bed. They read the story about Jesus dying on the cross. When they were finished, Sheryl said, "Too bad that Jesus had to suffer so much. I wish He hadn't died on the cross. I wish it had never happened." Joey said that she was wrong about that. What, do you suppose, made Joey say that?

3. Uncle Henry came to visit at Ricky's home. The first thing Ricky noticed when Uncle Henry arrived was the little golden cross on the lapel of his coat. After a while Ricky asked Uncle Henry why he wore that cross. Uncle Henry answered, "To show people that I am a Christian. You remember, Christ died on the cross to save us, and this shows that I believe in Him." Ricky didn't think he would like to wear a cross because that was such a cruel death. He would rather wear a cheerful little flower. Do you think Ricky was right?

JESUS IS CROWNED WITH GLORY

 Every boy and girl knows that hard work becomes much easier if you know there will be a reward for your work when it is finished. Jesus experienced something like this too. His Father promised Him great glory after His suffering and death were past. Jesus looked forward to this and it gave Him strength. He received this glory when He rose from the dead, ascended to heaven, and sat down at the Father's right hand. Christ's glory will become perfect when He returns at the end of time. Once He carried the cross. Now He wears the crown.

There are many stories about people who rose from rags to riches. You know, the Cinderella kind of stories, about servants who became landlords, about little people who became famous.

What boy doesn't dream once in a while about some day becoming President of the United States or Prime Minister of Canada? Such dreams can come true.

You remember Abraham Lincoln. He was born in a little log cabin in Illinois and grew up as a poor boy in Kentucky. But after much hard work he was elected President of the nation.

You also remember David the shepherd boy, who became King of Israel. After many dangers and hardships he received the crown.

The lives of such people prove that God can do great things with humble people.

What reward did the Father promise Jesus for finishing the work of salvation?

The greatest "rags-to-riches" story is in the Bible. It is the life of Jesus. Jesus' birth was more humble than that of any other person who was ever born. He had greater sufferings than any other person who ever lived. He rose to greater power and glory than any other person who has ever lived. He is now Lord and Master of everything in heaven and on earth.

Jesus now wears the crown of glory. This is His reward for living and dying in obedience to His Father's will. It is the crown of victory given to Him after the battle was won. While He was suffering and dying as the humble Servant of God, He kept His eye on the reward that was waiting for Him. This gave Him strength to keep going.

At each step in Jesus' suffering there was a reward to which He looked forward. When He was dying on the cross, He knew His Father would raise Him from the dead. When He left behind the glories of heaven and came to earth, He knew His Father would one day welcome Him back to glory. When He stepped down from His throne to become a Servant, He knew His Father would one day give Him a place at His own right hand. When men treated Him shamefully, He knew that He would one day return upon the clouds of heaven to judge all men.

Jesus had to travel this road through suffering to glory. For there is no victory without battle, no crown without a cross.

First, step by step Jesus went downward. Then, step by step Jesus went upward.

Here is a little picture of the steps downward and upward in Jesus' life:

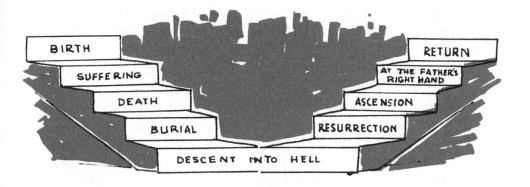

The turning point came on Easter Sunday. Jesus arose with a glorified body, never to die again. This was the beginning of glory for Jesus. Then, step by step, He climbed higher and higher up the ladder of glory and power.

The resurrection proves that the Father was satisfied with Jesus' work of salvation. This great miracle was God's way of saying "Well done!" to Jesus.

The two men going to Emmaus did not understand the resurrection of Jesus on that first Easter Sunday evening. They thought Jesus was still dead, and that they had lost Him forever. But then Jesus joined them. He walked along as the Stranger. He talked with them. He opened to them the Bible to show that the Savior had to suffer death in order to enter His glory. As they were sitting at supper, He opened their eyes. Suddenly they saw that this Stranger was really their Master. He had conquered death. Now He was their living Lord. They hurried back to Jerusalem with burning hearts and mouths eager to tell the good news.

What is Jesus doing now as He lives in heavenly glory?

Forty days after the resurrection, Jesus ascended to heaven. What a homecoming that must have been! The Father gave Him a place of honor and authority. Now, as Jesus had promised, He is getting ready for the day of His return. Then His glory on earth will become as perfect as it now is in heaven.

Some men, when they rise to great glory and power, use their authority in selfish ways. They try to get everything for themselves and make everyone else their slaves.

But Jesus does not act this way. Jesus went back to His heavenly home because He could help us more by going there than by staying here. What are some of the things Jesus is doing for us in heaven today? Let us mention three:

1. JESUS NOW MAKES US SHARE IN HIS WORK OF SALVATION. He finished that work while He was on earth. Nothing can be added to it. But now, every day, Jesus takes the blessings that He has earned and gives them to us. It is something like a doctor who discovers a new medicine. For this medicine to do some good, the doctor cannot leave it in his laboratory, but must give it to sick people to heal them. Jesus works something like that. First, while He was on earth, He made the cure for sin. Now, from heaven, He makes that cure ours.

2. JESUS NOW RULES THE WORLD ACCORDING TO GOD'S PLAN. On the cross Jesus won the victory over Satan. Satan cannot stand in Jesus' way. Jesus is now Ruler of the universe. In love and power He makes all things work together for good for His people. He also sends ministers and missionaries to preach the gospel. He sends teachers to teach us about the Father's world in which we live. He helps us serve Him with our lives.

3. JESUS NOW PRAYS FOR US EVERY DAY. When we pray, Jesus takes our prayers and makes them perfect. Then He prays our prayers for us before His Father. That is why we pray "in Jesus' name" and "for Jesus' sake."

> *Jesus has one more great work to do before everything is perfect. What is that work?*

Before Jesus returned to heaven, He said that He would come back again. He is now getting ready for that great day.

There is still a lot of wickedness left in the world. But in the end Jesus will make all things like new. To do this, He is planning to come back as the holy Judge and the mighty King.

That will be a wonderful day for all His people. If we believe in Him and love Him, we have nothing to fear but can look forward to everything good.

When He comes He will lock Satan and all his followers in the prison-house of hell. They will never be able to trouble us anymore.

Then He will give us a new earth under a new heaven, where we can enjoy a wonderful life and live forever with our God and Savior.

PRAYER

Lord Jesus, how happy I am to know that Thy saving work is finished and the victory is won. Look down upon me from heaven and please give me all the blessings of Thy great salvation. Rule over my life, so that I may do Thy will. When I die, take me to heaven so that I may live with Thee in glory forever. At Thy coming again I want to be on Thy side. Father in heaven, hear my prayer for Jesus' sake. Jesus my Savior, pray for me. Holy Spirit, fill my life with praise and thanksgiving. In Jesus' name, Amen.

BIBLE VERSE

This week's Bible verse and last week's Bible verse belong together. So they should be learned together. First review last week's Bible verse (Philippians 2:8). Then learn this week's Bible verse (Philippians 2:9-11).

Wherefore also God highly exalted him, and gave unto him the name which is above every name; that in the name of Jesus every knee should bow, of things in heaven and things on earth and things under the

*earth, and that every tongue should confess that Jesus
Christ is Lord, to the glory of God the Father.*
Philippians 2:9-11

THINKING IN BLACK-ON-WHITE

1. How does David's life show that God can do great things with humble people by leading them through suffering to glory?
2. During His sufferings, what did Jesus look forward to that gave Him strength to keep going? Read Hebrews 12:2.
3. What rewards did the Father promise to give Jesus after His suffering and death were finished? See John 17:5.
4. What does the resurrection prove about Jesus' work?
5. What is Jesus doing now as He sits in glory at the Father's right hand? See John 14:2, 3 and Hebrews 7:25 and Revelation 11:15.
6. How will Jesus make His glory perfect when He comes again?

QUESTIONS AND ANSWERS FOR MEMORY WORK

1. **What reward did Jesus receive for all His suffering?**
Jesus received the crown of glory because He won the victory over sin.
2. **What do we say in the Apostles' Creed about Jesus' reward of glory?**
In the Apostles' Creed we say: "The third day He arose from the dead; He ascended into heaven, and sitteth at the right hand of God the Father Almighty; from thence He shall come to judge the living and the dead."
3. **What does Jesus' resurrection mean?**
Jesus' resurrection means that the Father was satisfied with our Savior's finished work.
4. **What work is Jesus now doing from heaven?**
From heaven Jesus gives us the blessings of His salvation, rules over our lives, and prays for us.

5. **What will Jesus do when He comes again?**

When Jesus comes again He will judge all men, destroy all evil, and give His people a new life with Him in glory forever.

WHAT DO YOU THINK ABOUT IT?

1. Every day at Ken's house someone read a Bible story at one of the meals. Ken loved these stories. He relived them in his mind. You could tell it by that faraway look on his face at Bible story time. But, if Ken could make just one wish, he knew what it would be. He often wished that Jesus had stayed on earth and not returned to heaven. Then, so Ken thought, he would be able to go and see Him, and talk with Him, and listen to Him. Ken thought it was just too bad that Jesus had to leave us and go back to heaven. Was Ken right?

2. Sandra sometimes played with a neighborhood girl named Joan. Joan was from a Roman Catholic family. Sandra found out from Joan that Joan's family prayed to Mary the mother of Jesus, to ask Mary to pray for them. One evening as Sandra was lying in bed, after her bedtime prayer, she turned to her older sister Susan and asked, "Why don't we pray to Mary?" Suppose that you were Susan. What would you answer?

3. Many times, as Frank was sitting in church, he would hear the minister end his prayer with these words, "Come, Lord Jesus, come quickly." This thought always made Frank feel a little uneasy. After all, he was only ten years old. He wanted some time to grow up and become a great scientist. The minister could say that quite easily, because he was older. But Frank was young. Oh, yes, Frank wanted Jesus to come back all right, some day, but not too soon. What do you think about Frank's ideas?

THE ROAD DOWN AND THE ROAD UP

A Review Lesson

In the past six lessons we have followed two roads. They both go downhill, and they both go uphill.

The first road downhill is a sad road. It leads from beautiful, happy Paradise in the Garden of Eden. There Adam sinned against God and spoiled the happiness and beauty of Paradise. Adam and Eve had to leave the Garden of Eden and they led all men—you and me too—into sin's darkness.

The road down led to sadness. Cain killed his brother. Wars came. There was sickness, pain and suffering. It looked as if Satan and his evil angels were winning the battle.

But God did not leave Adam and Eve alone and helpless in the black midnight of sin. He made a promise. God said that He would send a great Savior who would defeat sin, Satan and the powers of darkness.

Gradually, over the centuries, God told His people more and more about the Savior who would conquer Satan and his armies. That Savior was King Jesus.

Jesus followed the road down too. But He did it because God so loved us that He sent His Son. He sent Him down to us who were lost in sin's darkness.

Down the road from heaven's glory to Bethlehem's cattle shed—down the dusty roads to seek and to save lost sinners like you and me. Jesus went all the way down to the death of a criminal on a cross. And there in the darkness He conquered sin and death and Satan. Jesus won the battle!

Now the road was up. God raised His Son from the grave, showing that Jesus had won the victory, that His work was well done. Sad disciples were made glad when they saw their risen Savior. Now they understood why King Jesus had to die in order to conquer sin and be able to wear the crown.

THE ROAD DOWN AND THE ROAD UP

JESUS IN
HEAVEN'S GLORY...

JESUS REIGNS
IN HEAVEN'S
GLORY

... CAME DOWN.

...IN A LOWLY
MANGER.

HE LOOKS
FORWARD TO BEING
WITH CHRIST

BECAME A
SERVANT...

SUFFERED

ASCENDED
INTO HEAVEN

AND

DIED

THE CHRISTIAN NOW
SEEKS TO LIVE
THE NEW LIFE

MAN IN
PARADISE...

AROSE FROM
THE DEAD

SINNED
AND
FELL -

JESUS CHRIST
FREED MAN
FROM SIN

INTO

SINS   DARKNESS

Later they saw Jesus disappear into the clouds as He went on the road up to His heavenly home. In heaven He now rules. As our victorious King He helps us win the victory over sin. He promises us that we too will one day join Him at the end of the road upward. He will return, and then we will live with Him forever in the new heaven and the new earth.

What a wonderful Savior is Jesus my Lord!

PRAYER

Dear King Jesus, I cannot understand the love that made Thee leave heaven's glory to come down to earth. But I thank Thee for taking the road down to rescue me. I confess my sins and my need of Thy saving power. Help me to show to other people the love that Thou hast shown to me. Help me to be a servant to others. And help me to win the victory over sin in my life. I thank Thee that I may pray in Thy name, Amen.

REVIEW QUESTIONS

These questions will help you to review what you have learned.

1. What is sin?
2. Why do we need a mighty Savior?
3. How was King David like King Jesus?
4. Was it an easy thing for Jesus to leave heaven and come to Bethlehem's manger?
5. Why does the Bible call Jesus a Servant?
6. What kind of people did Jesus come to help? (Rich ones? Poor ones? Common working people? Famous people?)
7. How can you follow Jesus' example as a humble servant?
8. What reward did God promise Jesus after His suffering and death was finished?
9. What is Jesus doing in heaven now?
10. What will Jesus do when He comes again?

THE HOLY SPIRIT APPLIES SALVATION

We have learned how Jesus Christ left heaven's glory to come into this world. We have seen how He suffered and died for our sins. We have learned that He has conquered sin and death and Satan for us, and how He now rules at God's right hand. In this lesson we shall study about how the Holy Spirit brings into our lives all these blessings that Jesus has earned for us.

Nancy Sherman's father was a minister in a small new church. One Sunday morning there were three visitors in the audience. Reverend Sherman knew them. He had invited them. There was Jimmy Osborn, a high school student, his friend Patty Phillips, and Don Johnson, a boy who worked in a service station down the street. Reverend Sherman was very happy to see them there because they were not members of a church.

The Holy Spirit works through the preaching of the Word of God.

That morning Reverend Sherman's sermon was about a well-known Bible text, John 3:16. He explained how God so loved the world that He gave His only begotten Son to save sinners. He made it clear that all who believe in Jesus—all who trust Him—will never perish but will have everlasting life. At the end of the sermon he invited any one who wanted to know more about this wonderful promise of the Bible to talk with him about it.

After the service one of the three visitors came to Reverend Sherman and said, "I want to believe in Jesus Christ. I want to trust in Him, to put my faith in Him."

The other two young people slipped away from church as fast as they could.

About an hour later Reverend Sherman came home and told the family that one of the three visitors had come to him and had said that he wanted to believe in Jesus Christ.

Nancy asked, "Which one was it?"

Pastor Sherman replied, "It was Don Johnson, Nancy."

"How come he believed and the other two didn't? They all heard the same sermon from the Bible."

"That's right," said her father, "but not everyone who hears believes. What everyone heard in church this morning was the Holy Spirit calling people to believe. They heard that call coming from God's Word as it was preached."

He went on to explain why Don believed the Gospel message. He told a story about another preacher, the Apostle Paul. It went something like this:

"On a Sabbath day Paul was looking for a group to whom he could preach the Gospel. He heard that there was a group of women who met outside the city on a grassy slope by a river bank. There they would pray. They believed in God, but they had not heard about Jesus Christ. So Paul went there. He told them the good news, that God had sent His Son, Jesus Christ, into the world to die for sinners. And just as had happened in church that morning, one person believed. It was Lydia.

"Read Acts 16:14, Nancy, and then tell me why Lydia believed."

> *The Holy Spirit opens the heart of the sinner.*

Nancy read the verse (it is your memory verse). It had these words in it: "And a certain woman named Lydia . . . heard us: whose heart the Lord opened to give heed unto the things which were spoken by Paul."

There was the answer. The Lord opened the heart of Lydia, and He opened the heart of Don Johnson.

Reverend Sherman said, "You see, Nancy, the Holy Spirit speaks to all who hear the Word of God. But people are sinners and don't want to believe what the Bible teaches. They call it foolishness. But when someone does believe, it is because the Holy Spirit also comes into the heart of that person, and opens that hard heart."

"What does it mean to open a hard heart?" asked Nancy.

"Well, let's see, Nancy, sometimes your mother calls to you and you don't want to hear her. Maybe it's because you have been naughty or because she wants you to do some of your duties. It is something like that with sinners. They have done bad things and don't want to hear God or do what God wants them to do.

"But there are other times when you want to please your mother. Then you answer right away, don't you? The Holy

Spirit works something like that. He makes us want to listen to God's Word and believe it and do what it says. He changes us. That is what Jesus meant when He said to Nicodemus, 'Ye must be born again.' He meant that Nicodemus had to be changed so that he would become like a new person."

The Holy Spirit leads us to repent.

Reverend Sherman went on to explain that when a person's heart is changed he wants to love and serve God. Then he is also sorry for his sins. He repents of his sins. Nancy's father also explained why they called Don Johnson a *convert*.

The Holy Spirit leads us to conversion.

"You see that same word in convertible. A convertible is a car that can be changed or turned into a car without a roof. Don was changed too. He was converted by the work of the

Holy Spirit. Don said that he didn't want to live to please himself anymore, but that he wanted to live for Jesus. He didn't want to sin any more, but he wanted to live a holy life for God."

The Holy Spirit leads you also to faith, repentance and conversion.

You, dear reader, are a child of God, and the Holy Spirit works this way in your life too. Long ago when you heard the Bible stories on your mother's knee, you loved those stories and you believed them. The Holy Spirit was calling you through those stories. He calls you, too, through the sermons that are preached in church, and He calls you through your study of catechism right now.

The Holy Spirit also opened your heart so that you believed and trusted in God. And each day the Holy Spirit leads you. It is the Holy Spirit in your heart who leads you to pray to God each day. It is the Holy Spirit who makes you sorry for

your sins. It is the Holy Spirit who makes you want to live a better life for Jesus.

So you see, it is the Holy Spirit who gives you all the blessings that come to us from Jesus Christ.

PRAYER

Dear heavenly Father, I thank Thee for the gift of Thy Son, Jesus Christ.

Dear Jesus, I thank Thee for what Thou hast done to save me from sin and death and Satan.

Dear Holy Spirit, I thank Thee for opening my heart to receive that gift. Guide me each day so that I may turn away from evil ways, and seek to do what is good. In Jesus' name and for His sake, Amen.

BIBLE VERSE

And a certain woman named Lydia, a seller of purple, of the city of Thyatira, one that worshipped God, heard us: whose heart the Lord opened to give heed unto the things which were spoken by Paul.

Acts 16:14

THINKING IN BLACK-ON-WHITE

Finish these sentences.

1. Sinners do not believe the Word of God because . . . .
2. Sinners who hear the Word of God and believe do so because the Holy Spirit . . . .
3. To repent of my sins means that I . . . .
4. Conversion means . . . .

QUESTIONS AND ANSWERS FOR MEMORY WORK

1. **By what means does God give you faith in Jesus Christ?**
   God gives me faith in Jesus Christ by means of His Word and Spirit.

2. **How does the Holy Spirit lead you to faith in Jesus Christ?**

The Holy Spirit leads me to faith in Jesus Christ by opening my heart and mind so that I hear and answer the call of the Word of God.

3. **How does the Holy Spirit change your life?**

The Holy Spirit changes my life as He leads me each day to be truly sorry for my sins, to trust in Jesus, and to want to live a life that is pleasing to God.

WHAT DO YOU THINK ABOUT IT?

1. Nancy Sherman (who was in our story) asked her father, "Daddy, I don't think I was ever suddenly converted like Don Johnson was. Am I converted?"

How do you think Reverend Sherman answered Nancy?

2. When the minister came over for a visit he asked Paul these questions:

Do you ever do things that are wrong?

Paul's answer:

How do you feel about it when you do things that are wrong?

Paul's answer:

What are you doing to become a better Christian boy?

Paul's answer:

You notice that Paul's answers are left out. But the minister said to him after he answered the questions, "Your answers show that the Holy Spirit is working in your heart, Paul."

What do you think Paul's answers might have been?

Lesson 16

LIFE'S HARDEST QUESTION

"Believe on the Lord Jesus, and thou shalt be saved, thou and thy house."

Acts 16:31

What is the hardest question that every person has to solve? Maybe you would say it has something to do with school. School can have its problems, all right, but there are bigger problems than these. For example, what are you going to do with your life? What are you going to be? Whom will you marry? These are problems. But we still haven't mentioned the hardest one of all. This lesson is about that problem.

What is life's hardest question?

The hardest question of all is this: How shall I become right with God? Maybe that doesn't sound like such a big problem to you. But it will if you think about it.

There is a day coming when you and all of your friends, your parents, and everyone who ever lived are all going to stand before a holy Judge. Each of us will hear that Judge give His verdict. There can be only two verdicts. He will say:

"Guilty. Take this one out of My presence forever, to the place of never ending suffering."

Or He will say:

"Not guilty. Enter into the perfect joy and happiness of your heavenly home, and live with Me forever."

Which verdict will be yours? Let's see if we can answer that question.

First of all, we have to know who the Judge is. He is the Lord Jesus Christ. God has said, "Be ye holy, for I the Lord your God am holy." He says, "Be perfect. Love Me with all your heart. Don't disobey Me at all, for that is sin, and the person who sins shall surely die." God also says, "The wages of sin is death."

Perhaps you are ready to say, "Well, if the verdict is going to be guilty for everyone who disobeys God—even just one of His laws—then I'm going to be found guilty."

And you would surely be right—if that was all there was to it. You would be more right than most people in the world. Most people think that if they try very hard to live a good life, then God will say to them, "Not guilty." But that isn't what the Bible teaches. The Word of God says that no man can be saved by his good works. Even our best works fall very far short of the love God asks of us. And if we sin in even one small thing, it shows that we really love ourselves better than we love God.

Some days you will try to be good. Everything goes well for almost the whole day. But maybe after dinner you lose your temper and get angry. You say a mean thing. We just can't be perfect, no matter how hard we try. How can I be right with God—how can I be found not guilty of breaking His law? That is a hard question, isn't it?

Can we get right with God by doing good works?

When Martin Luther was a young man he tried to solve this problem. His church taught him that he could be saved by

doing good works. So he got busy. For he had also learned all about how sinners would be cast out of God's presence forever, and punished in hell.

Young Martin decided to live in a monastery. That is a place with a high stone wall around it where men live to get away from the rest of the world. Martin Luther thought that if he went to such a place, he would not have so much chance to sin, and he could spend all his time doing good things.

While he was there he kept busy all day doing good things. He mopped the floors. He stayed up all night to pray. He would go without food for a long time. He helped the other men in every way he could. He worked so hard at trying to be good that he became very sick and almost died.

But no matter how hard he tried, he still was terribly worried. In the middle of the night he would be frightened awake by a nightmare in which he heard the voice of Jesus saying, "You are guilty, *guilty*, GUILTY." He thought Jesus was angry with him because he had not done enough good works to be saved.

One day Martin Luther was reading in the book of Romans and he came to the words, "The righteous shall live by faith" (Romans 1:17).

"What does that mean?" he said to himself. "Must I not live by good works? Isn't that the way to get right with God?"

We get right with God by faith in Jesus Christ.

Slowly he began to understand what that little verse meant. It turned out to be the key to answer the question, How shall I become right with God? The answer was, Not by good works, but by faith. What does this mean?

Let us think again of ourselves standing before the righteous and holy Judge.

"Not guilty," says the Lord. How can that be? I *am* guilty. I know that I have sinned, and that even the best things I do are far from perfect.

But we did not tell everything about the Judge. We said that God *hates sin,* but we must also say that God *loves the person,* even though he sins. The Bible says that while we were yet sinners, Christ died for us. God so loves sinners like us that He sent His Son to die for us, to save us by taking the terrible punishment that we deserve and by living a perfect life for us. These are things we could never do ourselves.

Well, if Jesus has taken the punishment for my sins, and if He has lived a perfect life for me, then what is left for me to do in order to be right with God? The answer is simple, and it is found in your memory verse, "Believe on the Lord Jesus, and thou shalt be saved" (Acts 16:31).

What does it mean to have faith in the Lord Jesus Christ?

What does it mean to believe in the Lord Jesus Christ? It means that I put all of my hope, all of my trust, all of my faith,

in Him and His salvation. I don't trust in my own good works or think that I can earn my way to heaven. I don't think I can get right with God all by myself—by what I do. No, I believe that Jesus did all this for me. I believe that He took the punishment I deserved. I believe that He suffered and died for my sins. I believe that His blood cleanses me from all my sins.

If you believe all of this, then a wonderful thing happens. God credits to your account all that Jesus did. If you have some money in the bank, then you can understand this. God takes what Jesus has done and He puts it under your name—He puts it on your account. Jesus paid for your sins. He bought everlasting life for you. He lived a perfect life for you. That is all put on your account in God's heavenly bank. How rich you are! How rich God's love is!

We started this lesson by saying that life's hardest question is this: How shall I become right with God? Now you have the answer to that question. Have you found that answer for yourself? You can know it right now, if you don't know it already. You don't have to wait until Jesus comes to judge the world. You can know right now that you are "not guilty," that you are right with God. How can you know? Pray the words of this prayer with all your heart and believe them:

PRAYER

Dear Jesus, I thank Thee that Thou hast died for my sins. I thank Thee that Thou hast lived a perfect life for me. I confess all my sins. I admit that I can't live a perfect life. All of my faith, all of my hope is in Thee and what Thou hast done for me. Wash me, and I shall be whiter than snow. Help me to love Thee and serve Thee all the days of my life. For Jesus' sake, Amen.

BIBLE VERSE

Believe on the Lord Jesus, and thou shalt be saved, thou and thy house.

Acts 16:31

THINKING IN BLACK-ON-WHITE

1. What is life's hardest and most important question? See Job 9:2.

2. How do many people in the world think they can get right with God? What did the rich young ruler think? Read Luke 18:18-27.

3. How did Martin Luther first try to get right with God?

4. How did Martin Luther finally get right with God?

5. What does it mean to have faith in Jesus Christ?

6. What did Jesus do for us? See I Corinthians 15:3-4 and Romans 5:8-10.

QUESTIONS AND ANSWERS FOR MEMORY WORK

1. **Can any of us become right with God by our good works?**
   No, we cannot become right with God by our good works, because even our best works are spoiled by sin.

2. **How can you become right with God?**
   I can become right with God only through faith in Jesus Christ.

3. **What happens when you put your faith in Jesus Christ?**
   When I put my faith in Jesus Christ, God forgives all my sins and I am no longer guilty, but right with God.

WHAT DO YOU THINK ABOUT IT?

1. Betty was in the fifth grade. One of her classmates was Judy Watkins. Judy was a very nice girl. She studied hard. She never said bad words. She was kind and helpful to others. But she did not believe in Jesus Christ. Should Betty say anything to Judy? What would you say?

2. Larry and Phil were talking about the story of Martin Luther that they had read in the lesson.

   Larry said, "I don't understand that story. Luther tried as hard as he could to be good, and it didn't help him a bit. My folks are always telling me to try to be good. Well, if it didn't help Martin Luther, why should I try?"

   If you were Phil, how would you answer Larry?

LIVING FOR JESUS

LIVING FOR JESUS IN WHAT WE
—DO
—SAY
—THINK

Do you ever ask yourself, "Why should I live as a Christian? And how should I live as a Christian?" Both of these are very important questions. This lesson will help you find answers to these questions. Did you ever stop to think that the name *Christian* has the name *Christ* in it? Therefore being a Christian means living the way Christ wants us to live. How does Christ want us to live? Why does He want us to live in a Christian way? Let's find out.

What does it mean to be a good boy or a good girl?

Every summer Allen Van Dyke looked forward to spending a week at Uncle Dick's farm. Then he could play with his favorite cousin Tom. There were so many exciting things to do. Allen could hardly wait.

Finally the day came. Uncle Dick drove up with his red truck. Allen put his suitcase in the back. Mother talked with Uncle Dick a while. Allen wished she would stop talking, so they could get going. Finally she did stop talking.

Then mother turned to Allen. She had saved a few words for her boy. Allen knew just what she would say. She kissed Allen good-bye, and added, "Listen to Aunt Jenny, and do what Uncle Dick says. Don't forget your prayers, *and be a good boy.*"

That was what Mother and Dad always said. Usually Allen hardly heard it. But this time it was different. Later that day as he played on the farm he could still hear those words, *"and be a good boy."* Allen wondered just what it meant to be a good boy.

What reasons do we have for trying to be good?

Boys and girls want to do the right things. But there are many different reasons for trying to be good.

Sometimes we try to be good because we don't want to be disciplined. If Allen were naughty, Uncle Dick might spank him or even send him home.

Sometimes we try to be good because we expect a reward. If Allen were a good boy, Uncle Dick might let him take a kitten along when he went home on Saturday.

Sometimes we try to be good because we don't want our friends to get bad ideas about us. If Allen did not behave well, Tom might not want to play with him.

Sometimes we try to be good because we love our parents and want to please them. If Allen did naughty things, he knew it would hurt his parents' feelings.

Which of these is the best reason for being good?

What does Jesus teach us about why we should try to be good?

Jesus wants us to be good too. This is the best reason of all for being good. When Jesus talks about being good, He means that we should live in a way pleasing to God—in a Christian way. You remember the Sermon on the Mount from Matthew 5, 6 and 7, don't you? In this Sermon Jesus tells us many things about living as Christians.

But why should we try to live as Christians? Jesus gives us three reasons why.

1. One reason is to show that Christ lives in us. In Matthew 7:16 we read that "by their fruits ye shall know them." Would

you expect to find apples growing on a poison upas tree? Of course not. Apples come from apple trees, and upas juice from the poison upas tree. You can tell what kind of tree it is by the fruit it gives. That is the way in our lives too, says Jesus. You can tell what a person is by the way he lives and the good or bad things he does.

Think of yourself as a tree, a Christian tree. What if there were unchristian fruits coming from the tree of your life? That would not be good, would it? If we call ourselves Christians, people should be able to see that we are Christians by the way we live.

This is one reason why we should live in a Christian way.

2. Jesus gives us another reason in the parable about the two builders. You remember how the one man built his house

upon the rock, and the other man built his house upon the sand. When the rains came down, and the floods came up, and the winds blew hard, the house built on sand caved in. But the house built on the rock stood firm.

The wise man is like a person who hears Jesus' words and obeys them. The foolish man is like a person who hears Jesus'

words, but forgets them. To live as a Christian means listening to Jesus' words and obeying them.

Think of your life as a house—a Christian house—that you are building with your deeds and words and thoughts. You don't want the house of your life to cave in, do you? Then you must live in a good way. This means obeying the words of Jesus.

Now we have a second reason why we should live a good Christian life.

3. Jesus gave us a third reason in His healing of the ten lepers. In a certain village ten lepers came to Jesus and cried, "Master, have mercy on us!" Jesus sent all ten upon their way to be healed. But only one returned to thank Jesus. What happened to the other nine?

All of us were like lepers, unclean because of our sins. But Jesus has healed us from the sickness of our sins. Now what does Jesus expect of us? Forget His goodness, like the nine lepers? No, He expects us to be thankful to Him and to show it by living for Him.

These are three good reasons for trying to be really good in a Christian way. Can you remember them? Let's review them briefly:

1. So that we can show by our fruits that we are Christians.
2. So that we can keep the house of our life standing firm.
3. So that we can show our thankfulness to Jesus.

What does Jesus teach us about how we should be good Christians?

This week would be a good time to read the Sermon on the Mount. There Jesus teaches us many things about how to live as Christians. Let's look at just three rules that Jesus gives us in this sermon.

1. He teaches us how to live for Him by the way we *speak* to others. Sometimes we tell lies, don't we? Sometimes we swear when we say, "Cross my heart and hope to die." Jesus hears such bad talk. It displeases Him. He says that our speech should be "Yes" or "No," and anything more than this is evil. Jesus means to tell us, "Always tell the truth." This is how we live for Him in our words. Read Matthew 5:33-37.

2. Jesus teaches us how to live for Him by the way we *think* about other people. Some people think it is all right if we love our friends and hate our enemies. But Jesus wants our minds to be pure. He says, "Love your enemies, and pray for them that persecute you." This is how we live for Him in our thoughts. Read Matthew 5:43-48.

3. Jesus teaches us how to live for Him by the way we *act* toward other people. Read the Golden Rule in Matthew 7:12. This is our Bible verse for this week. Here Jesus puts all our duties toward other people in one little verse. We want other people to be good to us, don't we? "Well," says Jesus, "then you should be good to them too." This means many things. It means helping your mother in the kitchen. Helping your father take care of the yard. Visiting a sick friend to cheer him up. Keeping your tongue from telling lies and speaking evil of others. Doing good to those who are mean to you, and loving them. These are some ways we live for Jesus.

When we don't live this way, we must pray to Jesus to forgive our sins. When we do live this way we should be happy.

PRAYER

Father in heaven, I really want to be good, even though I am often naughty. I really want to live as a Christian, even though I am often unkind to others. Teach me to know what is good and what is bad. Help me to do what is right and true. Guide me in my words and thoughts and deeds to live for Jesus. Show me how to obey the Golden Rule. Forgive my sins and make me a happy Christian. In Jesus' name, Amen.

BIBLE VERSE

All things therefore whatsoever ye would that men should do unto you, even so do ye also unto them.

Matthew 7:12

THINKING IN BLACK-ON-WHITE

1. From the story in the lesson, what would Allen think it meant to be a good boy?

2. The lesson mentions four reasons why boys and girls often try to be good. What are they? Which one of these is the best reason? Which one of these is the poorest reason?

3. What three reasons does Jesus give for living in a Christian way?

4. Give examples of how we can live for Jesus in our words and thoughts and deeds. Complete the following sentences:

   a. We show we are Christians by the way we *speak* when we....

   b. We show we are Christians by the way we *think* when we....

   c. We show we are Christians by the way we *act* when we....

QUESTIONS AND ANSWERS FOR MEMORY WORK

1. **What does being a Christian mean for our lives?**

   To be a Christian means to live for Jesus.

2. **How do we live for Jesus?**

   We live for Jesus by hearing and obeying His Word.

3. **Why should you live as a Christian?**

   I should live as a Christian to show that Christ lives in me, and that I obey Him, and to show my thankfulness to Jesus.

4. **How can you show to others that you are a Christian?**

   I can show to others that I am a Christian by living for Jesus in my words and thoughts and deeds.

WHAT DO YOU THINK ABOUT IT?

1. It seemed as if Paul and Jim were always hungry. About the middle of the morning they wanted a cookie. "Ask your mother," suggested Paul. "Aw, we don't have to do that," said Jim. "She's across the street at Smith's. She will never know about it. Let's just take some." "But what if we get caught?" asked Paul. "Then we will both be punished," he added. So they decided to wait until Jim's mother returned. Did Jim and Paul do the right thing? Was their reason for not stealing the cookies a good one?

2. David and Ken were planning to go on a two-day camp-out. There would be many strange boys at the camp. They wondered just how they should act at camp. "Let's just act like everybody else does," suggested Ken. "I guess that is the best way," replied David. "We can forget all about the way we do things at home. Then no one will find out that we are Christians. It doesn't matter if we skip praying for a few days. We can just talk in any old way and can do as we please. We'll have a blast." The boys didn't know it, but mother was listening to their conversation. What do you suppose she would say about this? Who else was listening? What would He say?

GOD'S PERFECT LAW

Tommy looked at the words of the song they were singing in church. It began, "How I love thy Law, O Lord! Daily joy its truths afford." He thought to himself, "How can someone love the law? How does it give me joy?" Maybe you too wonder as Tommy did. This lesson tries to answer Tommy's questions.

"Slow." "Speed Limit 25 Miles per Hour." "Do Not Pass." "Speed Limit 65 Miles per Hour." You have seen such signs along the highway.

There are traffic laws to help people who are driving cars. When people don't obey those laws they may have trouble. Every day people are killed on the highways because someone does not obey the law. Maybe you have been in an accident caused by someone who broke a traffic law.

Traffic laws are good laws, although some people don't seem to think so. And there are many other good laws that help us in different ways.

Do you know that your Bible is a law book? As you read it, you find many laws that tell you how you should live. The laws in the Bible are God's laws. They are the rules He has given us. God wants us to read them and to obey them, just as a good driver reads the signs and obeys them.

Are God's laws good? Do they help us?

Sometimes people make laws that aren't good. King Nebuchadnezzar made a bad law when he said that everyone had to bow down to an idol. You will remember that the three young men would not obey this law. They said they had to obey God's perfect law instead.

How, do you think, did Shadrach, Meshach, and Abednego know so surely that God's law was right and that the king's law was wrong? After all, the king was ready to throw them into a burning furnace if they didn't obey his law. Wasn't it because they knew that God was their good and loving Father? They knew that the laws God gives to His children are true and good. From the time they were little children they had obeyed God's law, and they always found that it was good to obey God's commandments. A heavenly Father who is good and perfect never tells His children to do things that are bad for them. Read Daniel 3 and see how right those three young men were.

God's laws are fair and just.

On the playground we often hear someone say, "You are not playing fair." Or, "It isn't fair that the boys get to play with the good ball all the time." Doesn't someone often spoil your game because they want to play by rules that aren't fair and just?

God's law is never that way. It is always fair and just. If everyone obeyed God's commandments, our lives would be more like a game where everyone obeys rules that are fair. But the world isn't that way, is it? People break God's laws. They kill, steal, hate and lie. And then it becomes like a game where no one is fair. Everything is spoiled. Did you ever think how nice it would be if everyone obeyed God's laws?

God's laws help us.

Answer these questions to yourself. What happens to people who steal or lie or murder? What happens to people who are lazy and don't do their best? What happens to boys and girls who are mean to others? Do you think they have happy lives?

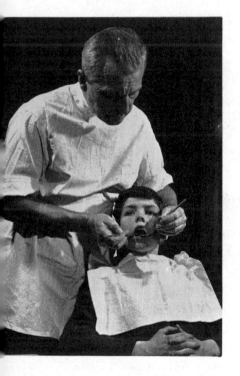

You see, if we don't obey God's laws, we will find trouble and not happiness. We just can't break God's laws and get away with it. This is true even in such little things as brushing our teeth. God tells us that we should take good care of our bodies. What happens if you don't keep your teeth clean? First a cavity, then a toothache, and then a visit to the dentist.

The Law teaches us that we are sinners. It tells us that we need Jesus as our Savior.

How do you know that you are a sinner? Isn't it in the same way that the driver of a car knows he is breaking the law? He sees a sign, "Speed Limit 25 Miles per Hour," and he is going 40 miles per hour. He knows he is going too fast because the sign says "25" and his speedometer says "40."

In the same way we know that we are sinners. God's laws are like traffic signs. As we are going along we say a mean thing, or we lie. Then we know that we have done wrong because in our mind we see the signs, "Thou shalt love thy neighbor" and "Thou shalt not bear false witness"—which means to lie. We know we are sinning. God's law tells us so.

This happens every day in different ways, doesn't it? But God will not set aside His Law. He will punish those who disobey it. The penalty must be paid. And so the Law teaches us that we need Jesus because we are never able to keep the Law perfectly.

We keep God's laws to show how thankful we are that Jesus died for our sins.

Mary's parents gave her a beautiful radio. She was so happy that she thanked them over and over. Not only that, she found herself helping mother with the dishes and other chores around the house. Mother didn't even have to ask. And when Mary was finished with one thing she asked if there was anything else she could do.

What made Mary act that way? Wasn't it because she was trying to show how thankful she was for the gift? In the same way we ask, What can I do to show how thankful I am to God for all He has done for me? Jesus gives us the answer. He says, "If you love me, you will keep my commandments."

PRAYER

Father in heaven, teach me to love Thy law. Help me to live in obedience to Thy commandments. I want to do this to show my thankfulness for the gift of Thy Son, Jesus Christ. In His name I pray, Amen.

BIBLE VERSE

I delight to do thy will, O my God;
Yea, thy law is within my heart.

Psalm 40:8

THINKING IN BLACK-ON-WHITE

1. Why can we trust that the laws of God are better than the laws of men? How did the three young men in Daniel chapter 3 know?

2. Show how we will be happier and healthier if we obey God's laws.

3. Make a list of five things that you find in the newspaper that would not have happened if everyone had obeyed God's laws.

4. How does the law of God teach us that we need Jesus as our Savior? What does Galatians 3:24 tell us?

5. What is the most important reason for wanting to obey God's laws? Read John 14:15, 21.

6. "Oh how love I thy law" (Psalm 119:97)! Why, do you think, did the man who wrote that verse love God's law?

QUESTIONS AND ANSWERS FOR MEMORY WORK

1. **How do you know that God's laws are good and holy?**
I know that God's laws are good and holy because they come from God, my loving Father, who is good and holy.

2. **Why is God's law good for everyone?**

God's law is good for everyone because it shows us the only right and happy way to live.

3. **How does God's law show you that you need Jesus as your Savior?**

God's law shows me that I need Jesus as my Savior by reminding me of my sins.

4. **Why do Christians want to keep God's law?**

Christians want to keep God's law to show thankfulness to God for His salvation.

WHAT DO YOU THINK ABOUT IT?

1. Some boys were talking about getting some firecrackers for the Fourth of July. One of them said that it was against the law. Another boy said, "That's not a good law. We don't have to obey it. The Bible doesn't say that we can't shoot off firecrackers."

   Would you agree that God's law doesn't say anything to those boys about shooting off some firecrackers?

2. Sally learned from reading her Bible lesson that people who obey God's laws live happier lives. She wondered about this. Her next-door neighbors had parties and often got drunk. When they did this they would laugh and make a lot of noise. They surely seemed happy. But they were breaking God's laws. There were also those older boys who raced their cars on the highway. They were breaking God's laws too. But they seemed to be having a good time. Sally asked her father about this. What do you think he said?

THE GREAT COMMANDMENT OF LOVE TO GOD

You remember the girl named Mary from your last lesson? By happily obeying her mother's commands she showed how thankful she was for her gift. This is an example of what God expects of us as Christians. He wants us to show our thanks to Him by obeying His laws. Where can we find God's laws? In the whole Bible, of course, but especially in the Ten Commandments. There He tells us very clearly how we should show our love and thanks to Him by obeying His will.

How did we get the Ten Commandments?

From the very beginning of the world God gave man His good laws. But they were not written down until the time of Moses. You remember how God visited with Moses on the top of Mount Sinai. There God talked with Moses for forty days and gave him the Ten Commandments. The commandments were written on two stone tablets. When Moses came down from the mountain, he read these commandments to the children of Israel so that they could learn how to obey God's laws.

Later, when Moses wrote the first five books of the Bible, he copied the Ten Commandments in two different places. Do you know where? Be sure to find out.

How are the Ten Commandments divided?

The Ten Commandments are divided into two parts, called the Two Tables of the Law. The First Table of the Law has in it the first four commandments, and the Second Table of the Law has in it the last six commandments.

In the First Table of the Law God tells us how to show our love to Him, and in the Second Table of the Law He shows us how to show our love to other people.

Why does God hold the first place in the Ten Commandments?

Once, on her birthday, Sandra said, "The most important persons in the world are I, myself, and me." This was very selfish. I am glad Sandra got over it the next day, for the Ten Commandments teach us to think about God first. He should always have first place, for He is the most important Person in our lives. Our highest goal in life should be to show our love and thanks to God. We do this by keeping His law.

What did Jesus teach us about the great commandment?

Jesus wants us to love the Father more than anybody and anything else in the world. He taught this clearly in His

answer to a certain proud Pharisee. This Pharisee tried to trick Jesus with the question, "Teacher, which is the greatest commandment in the law?" The Pharisees taught the people hundreds of different laws. This man hoped Jesus would get all mixed up. But Jesus silenced him by giving the only right answer, "Thou shalt love the Lord thy God with all thy heart, and with all thy soul, and with all thy mind. This is the great and first commandment." Read Matthew 22:34-40. Where have you heard these words before?

Jesus tied the first four commandments of the Law together in this one great commandment. Love is the one way to obey all God's laws. We must love Him first of all and above all and best of all. The first four commandments are four good helpers given by God to show us how to obey the great commandment of love. Let us look at these four commandments.

> *What does the introduction to the*
> *Ten Commandments teach us?*

I am Jehovah thy God, who brought thee out of the land of Egypt, out of the house of bondage. Exodus 20:2.

These words tell us that the Ten Commandments come from God, the Deliverer of His people. God saved His people Israel from slavery in Egypt. He saves us too from the slavery of Satan. These laws do not come from a cruel ruler. They are good laws that our heavenly Father gives to us, His children, so that we may know how to serve Him.

> *What does the first commandment*
> *teach us?*

Thou shalt have no other gods before me. Exodus 20:3.

This commandment tells us *whom* we must worship. When God gave this law, the nations around Israel served many gods. The Egyptians, with whom the children of Israel had lived, worshiped the sun, the River Nile, and many idols. They even

thought some animals were holy. When the Israelites moved into the land of Canaan, they met people who worshiped the idols Baal and Moloch and Asherah. God gave them this commandment to warn them against such wickedness. Jehovah reminded His people that He is the only true God. Nobody can be happy by serving idols and false gods.

Today in some parts of the world people still worship gods made of wood and stone and gold and silver. Some people who live around us make gods out of fun and money. Sometimes we, too, want a new bicycle or a new dress so badly that we forget our love to God. This is being very unthankful. God deserves our highest love. This is what Jesus taught us in His answer to Satan in the wilderness: "Thou shalt worship the Lord thy God, and him only shalt thou serve" (Matthew 4 verse 10).

What does the second commandment teach us?

Thou shalt not make unto thee a graven image. Exodus 20 verse 4.

This commandment teaches us *how* we should worship God. Some people think they can bring God closer to them by using images and idols to worship God. You remember how Israel tried to worship God by dancing around the golden calf. Remember how King Jeroboam made Israel bow down before the golden calves at Bethel and Dan. This is wrong, because God is so great that He can't be worshiped this way.

Today some people still believe in magic and good-luck charms. They think they can get good things by these superstitions.

God wants us to worship Him, not by things that men make, but with our hearts. When Jesus spoke to the Samaritan woman, He said, "God is a Spirit: and they that worship him must worship in spirit and truth" (John 4:24).

What does the third commandment teach us?

Thou shalt not take the name of Jehovah thy God in vain; for Jehovah will not hold him guiltless that taketh his name in vain. Exodus 20:7.

Cursing and swearing are two of the worst sins. God is holy, and His name is holy. When men use God's name in vain, they are attacking the holy God. There is a terrible punishment for this sin.

It hurts us, doesn't it, to hear people curse and swear? Would a person ever use his father's or mother's name that way? Yet some people do this every day with the name of God. We as children of God should never copy this terrible sin. How could we ever speak evil of the One we love the most! When we hear other people swear, we should tell them what a great sin this really is.

Jesus warns us against this sin when He says, "Swear not at all; neither by the heaven, for it is the throne of God; nor by the earth, for it is the footstool of his feet" (Matthew 5: 34, 35).

What does the fourth commandment teach us?

Remember the sabbath day, to keep it holy. Six days shalt thou labor, and do all thy work; but the seventh day is a sabbath unto Jehovah thy God: in it thou shalt not do any work. Exodus 20:8, 9.

Every day in our life belongs to God. Six days He wants us to work and play for Him. On Sunday He wants us to take time out from work and play in order to worship Him. Then we can learn to love God better by listening to the preaching of His Word. Then we can thank God by praying with His people in church. Our bodies need a day of rest. Our souls need time to worship. If we draw near to our Father on Sunday, then we can serve Him as His children better on Monday. This is the way to a happy life. This is the way to live to God's glory.

PRAYER

Father in heaven, I thank Thee for Thy good laws. Help me to understand Thy commandments. Teach me to show my thanks to Thee by doing Thy will. Open my heart to hear the great commandment, so that I may love Thee with all my heart and soul and mind and strength. In Jesus' name, Amen.

BIBLE VERSE

Thou shalt love the Lord thy God with all thy heart, and with all thy soul, and with all thy mind, and with all thy strength. Mark 12:30

THINKING IN BLACK-ON-WHITE

1. In which two chapters of the Bible can we find the Ten Commandments?
2. What is the difference between the First Table and the Second Table of the Law? Notice how Jesus divides the Ten Commandments (Matthew 22:37-40).
3. Why do the Ten Commandments give first place to loving God?
4. What does the introduction to the Ten Commandments teach us about God?
5. How does the first commandment teach us to love God above all?
6. What does the second commandment teach us about how we should worship God?
7. Why is it so sinful to break the third commandment?
8. How does the fourth commandment help us live a happy life?

QUESTIONS AND ANSWERS FOR MEMORY WORK

1. **Where do we find the Law of God?**
We find the Law of God especially in the Ten Commandments.

2. **How are the Ten Commandments divided?**
The Ten Commandments are divided into two parts, the first teaching us to love God above all, and the second teaching us to love our neighbors as ourselves.

3. **What does the First Table of the Law tell you about God?**
The First Table of the Law tells me that God is the only God and that He teaches me to obey His will thankfully by keeping His commandments.

WHAT DO YOU THINK ABOUT IT?

1. Sally had a girl friend, Jean, whose father was a missionary. Sometimes they would talk about living on the mission field. To Sally it seemed like a very hard life. Once she asked Jean, "Why does your father want to be a missionary?" "For many reasons, I guess," said Jean, "but he always says that the main reason is because he believes in the first commandment." What do you think Jean's father meant by that?

2. Some people, especially in the Roman Catholic Church, believe they should worship God through images and statues, so they set them up in their churches. Then people can use them to worship God. Perhaps you have seen such images and statues somewhere. What do you think about this?

3. Sometimes when Billy became very angry he would say the most awful things. In fact, he hardly knew what he was saying when he became really angry. At one such time he even swore by using God's name in vain. Billy's mother talked to him about this and reminded him of the words of the third commandment. "Aw," said Billy, "it isn't so bad. I really didn't mean it that way." Was Billy right?

Our Father

who art in Heaven
hallowed be thy Name thy kingdom
come thy Will be done on earth
as it is in Heaven.
Give us this day our daily bread
and forgive us our trespasses
as we Forgive them that
trespass against us + And lead
us not into temptation but deliver
us from evil: for thine is the
kingdom. the power. and the glory
for Ever and Ever

Amen

Lesson 20

LORD, TEACH US TO PRAY

Praying is talking to God. But when we talk to God, what should we say? The hardest thing about praying is knowing how we should pray and about what we should pray. The disciples of Jesus had this same problem. They once came to Jesus and asked, "Lord, teach us to pray." In this lesson we want to find out what the Bible says about how we should pray and what things we should pray for.

How did Jesus teach His disciples to pray?

The disciples of Jesus remembered that John the Baptist had taught his disciples to pray. They wanted Jesus to help them learn to pray. That is why they said, "Lord, teach us to pray."

Didn't the disciples know how to pray? Yes, but not very well. Many times they listened as Jesus prayed with them. Sometimes they watched Him pray all night. Jesus could pray better than anyone else in the world. Who could teach them the secret of how to pray and what to pray better than Jesus? So they said, "Lord, teach us to pray."

We must learn this too. Every Christian boy and girl is also a disciple of Jesus. You can pray too, can't you? But sometimes you don't know what to pray about. Sometimes you have to stop right in the middle of your prayers. Sometimes you can't seem to find the right words.

How do you learn to pray? By listening to others pray, don't you? When you hear your parents or your minister pray, perhaps you say to yourself, "I wish I could pray like that." Then you are really saying, "Lord, teach me to pray."

Jesus understood that all His disciples learn to pray by listening to prayers. So, when His disciples asked, "Lord, teach us to pray," He didn't give them a long speech about prayer. He did something far better. He taught them a prayer. Right there He said the Lord's Prayer. He showed them how to pray by doing it for them. They learned by listening to Jesus and using His words in their own prayers.

Do you understand now why there is a prayer in each one of these lessons? This is a good way to learn how to pray.

When we pray, must we always use the exact words of the Lord's Prayer? No, but from this perfect prayer we can learn what things we should pray for. The Lord's Prayer has two parts. In the first part we praise God for His greatness. In the second part we pray about our needs.

How should we pray about ourselves? Well, let's find out by listening to what Lee learned about praying.

How should we pray?
A day in Lee's life.

Lee sprang out of bed. Quickly he ran to the window. He pulled aside the curtain to let the summer sunshine in. It was a beautiful Saturday morning. Before getting dressed, Lee dropped to his knees and prayed. Sometimes he forgot, but this morning he remembered.

"I thank Thee, Lord, for watching over me during the night. What a wonderful morning Thou hast given!" Lee caught some good breakfast smells floating up the stairway. "I thank Thee for good food, and for Mother who makes fine meals, and for Daddy who earns money to buy it." Lee peeked around his bedroom a moment. "I thank Thee for a good house to live in, and for clothes." Suddenly Lee thought of his friend Billy and their plans for a hike. "I thank Thee for friends, for a healthy body so I can play, for fun things to do." Then he couldn't think of anything else, so he said, "For Jesus' sake, Amen."

In a minute Lee was downstairs. He kissed his mother and said, "Good morning." Daddy had already gone to work. So Lee sat down to eat with Mother and little sister Julie.

Mother always read a psalm at breakfast time. This morning she chose Psalm 25. (Why not read it yourself today?)

Mother explained that this psalm was really a prayer by David. After reading it she prayed for the family.

"Dear loving Father, please forgive our sins of yesterday." Lee remembered how Billy and he had teased some little girls. He felt bad about it. "Help us today to show that we are Christians by living for Jesus." Lee made up his mind to really try harder to be good today. "Bless Daddy as he works this morning. Help us to have a good time at our picnic with the Grovers this afternoon. Prepare our hearts for Sunday, so that we may truly worship Thee in church tomorrow. Bless Reverend Johnson and the other ministers as they get ready to preach." Lee was sort of glad Mother mentioned that. He had almost forgotten that tomorrow was Sunday. "Help all Thy people to understand the Bible and obey it. Bless Grandpa with his heart trouble. Be good to Mrs. Bradley in the hospital and make her better soon. Give Lee and Billy a good time on their hike. Help us and our children to love Thee always. In Jesus' name, Amen."

After breakfast Lee quickly washed and brushed his teeth. Almost on the run he snatched the lunch bag off the kitchen counter, said "Good-bye," and ran off to call for Billy.

That evening, after the morning hike and the afternoon picnic, Lee's family sat around the dinner table. Father read from the Bible story book. Then he reached for the Prayer Guide. For this day it said, "Pray for the mission work in Nigeria. Remember the missionaries, the doctors and nurses, the teachers and the African pastors. Ask God's blessing upon these young Christians as they try to build a new chapel."

Dad began his prayer. "Our Father who art in heaven." It seemed to Lee that Dad always knew just what to say when he prayed. He remembered the mission work in Africa. He even asked God's blessing upon the principal and teachers at school, even though it was vacation time. He prayed for better feeling between white people and Negroes. Then he prayed for the President. Father always prayed for a lot of things.

"Look in mercy upon our nation and the other nations of the world. Help us to work for peace on the earth. Help all the rulers to do Thy will. Make us truly thankful for being free people, and especially for being Christians. In Jesus' name, Amen."

Lee liked Dad's prayers, even though they sometimes seemed a little too long. He could see that Dad and Mom really knew how to talk to God. Nothing was too big or too small to pray about. I hope, Lee thought to himself, that someday I can pray like that.

What things should we pray for?
Another day in Lee's life.

The next day was Sunday. The whole family went to church, but Julie went down to the nursery. Before the service began, Lee read the bulletin. At the top of one page were these words: "All who enter this House of Prayer, remember to pray for him who leads in worship, for those who worship with you, and for yourself, so that we may praise God and receive His blessing." Lee thought about this during the silent prayer.

In his Sunday prayer Reverend Johnson prayed about many things—important and little things, even for people who don't

go to church. Just as Jesus did on the cross, He prayed even for His enemies. In his sermon the Pastor mentioned how Stephen prayed even for those who were stoning him to death.

All this made Lee wonder. After church he asked his mother

whether he could pray for anybody and about anything he had in mind. "Yes," his mother answered, "the Bible says we can pray about everything except those things that we know are against God's will."

Lee had learned a lot about praying those last two days. But most of all he learned to see the truth of Jesus' words in our Bible verse: "Verily, verily, I say unto you, If ye shall ask anything of the Father, he will give it you in my name" (John 16:23). The most important word in that text is the word *anything*. Remember this when you pray.

PRAYER

Lord, teach me to pray as I ought to pray. My prayers are weak and imperfect. But Thou art good and strong. Help me to find words to say what is in my heart. Make me a true disciple, so that I may freely talk to Thee in prayer about everything I have in mind. Father in heaven, hear and answer my prayers, for I pray in Jesus' name, Amen.

BIBLE VERSE

Verily, verily, I say unto you, If ye shall ask anything of the Father, he will give it you in my name.
John 16:23

THINKING IN BLACK-ON-WHITE

1. Why did Jesus' disciples ask, "Lord, teach us to pray"?
2. How did Jesus answer this request?
3. How can we learn to pray better?
4. What can we learn from Lee's morning prayer?
5. What could Lee learn from the things his mother said in her morning prayer?
6. Mention three things from the evening dinner prayer that show that Lee's father talked with God about many important things.
7. What did Lee learn from the prayer by the minister?

QUESTIONS AND ANSWERS FOR MEMORY WORK

1. **How did Jesus teach us to pray?**
   Jesus taught us to pray by His teachings, by showing us how He prayed, and by giving us the Lord's Prayer.

2. **What does the Lord's Prayer teach you about how you should pray?**
   The Lord's Prayer teaches me to praise God and to ask Him to satisfy all my needs.

3. **What things may you pray for?**
   I may pray for all the needs of my body and soul, and for all the needs of all men.

WHAT DO YOU THINK ABOUT IT?

1. At the Kamper home the whole family took part in meal-time prayers. Sometimes they would take turns praying. Once in a while they would have a chain prayer, beginning with Mother, with each child adding something, and Father closing the prayer. In his part of such a chain prayer Calvin, the ten-year-old, once asked God to help his baseball team with the championship game. Afterward Calvin's sister, Grace, said that we shouldn't talk about such things in our prayers. What do you think about this?

2. Jack was always having trouble at school with Buster Stengel, a big boy in the sixth grade. Almost every day they got into a fight. Twice both Jack and Buster were sent to the principal's office. Jack's parents talked with him about this problem several times. Jack said he didn't want to cause this trouble, and he really didn't like to fight with Buster all the time. But he didn't know what to do about it. "Have you ever prayed about it, Jack?" Father asked one evening. "Aw, that won't help," answered Jack. "What can God do about it anyway? He doesn't listen to these kind of things. He can't just make us love each other all at once, can He? Buster and I will have to settle this ourselves in our own way." Was Jack right about this?

THE ROAD OF THANKFUL LIVING

A Review Lesson

Do you remember our last review lesson? We talked about two roads down and two roads up. Jesus went on the one road, all the way down from heaven's glory to Calvary where He conquered sin for us. Then He rose from the dead, ascended into heaven, and now sits at the right hand of God. But He didn't leave us in sin's darkness. He makes it possible for us to walk a road that leads up. Our last six lessons have been about our walk on the upward road.

On the opposite page you can see a picture of that road. The picture is called The Road of Thankful Living. Let us go back through the six lessons we have studied. You will see how those lessons lead us along that upward road.

First we saw how the Holy Spirit leads us out of sin's darkness. The Holy Spirit opened the heart of Lydia so that she believed the good news that Jesus had died to save her from sin. The Holy Spirit gave her a new heart so that she wanted to live for Jesus. He turned her feet away from sinful paths and set her walking on the path that leads upward to God. The Spirit also made her sorry for her sins. She repented. The Holy Spirit does this in our lives too.

You see how the Holy Spirit set her feet so that she walked the road of faith. She believed and trusted in Jesus. And when she did this, God credited her account with all that Jesus had done for her. She was right with God. Everything that had happened in sin's darkness was forgiven. This is how we too get right with God.

When we walk the road of faith it is a happy road. Our hearts are filled with thanksgiving for what God has done for us. Now we want to live a new life. We want to show that we are Christians. We want our lives to be what God wants them to be. So we try to live as did the man who built his house on a rock. We listen to Jesus' words, and we try to obey them.

We learned that God has given us many signs to guide us as we walk the road of thankful living. He tells us how we can serve Him.

First we saw how Jesus taught us in the Sermon on the Mount.

Then we learned about God's laws. We saw that they are good and fair. They help us to lead a good and happy life. They show us how God wants us to live. God's laws also keep us out of the terrible ditches along the road. Those who don't follow the signposts of God's laws fall into those ditches.

The law of God does something else too. We are reminded of our sins because we don't always obey His law. When this happens we turn again to God, asking Him to forgive us for Jesus' sake. And we ask for all that we need to walk the road of thankful living. We do this by prayer—which is another signpost on our upward road.

We paid special attention to those guideposts that tell us how we must love God above all. As we go through life we are to worship and trust Him alone. We are never to worship idols, nor are we ever to swear. Every seventh day we are to rest along the way and worship Him.

And always we are to pray. We must ask God for all we need in order to walk the road of thankful living. We pray for others who are also walking that road and need God's help. We even pray for our enemies and for those who are still in sin's darkness. Prayer is one of the most important things we do on the upward road. We could never make it without God's help. When we pray, He answers our prayer and gives us all that we need to go onward.

Pray now for God's help as you walk the road of thankful living.

PRAYER

Heavenly Father, I thank Thee for putting my feet on the road of thankful living. Guide my footsteps along the way. Teach me to love Thee above all. Please help others who are walking the road. Open the hearts of people who are still in sin's darkness. Help me to show others the happy road of thankful living. In Jesus' name, Amen.

REVIEW QUESTIONS

1. Why do some people believe when they hear the Word of God, and why are there other people who don't believe?
2. Put in your own words what is meant by:
   a. Being born again.
   b. Repenting.
   c. Conversion.
3. Why can't we get right with God by trying to live a good life and doing good works?
4. What do you mean when you say that you have faith in Jesus Christ?
5. Why should you try to live a good life?
6. What are some ways in which you can show other people that you are a Christian?
7. Why does the Christian love God's law?
8. Mention three things that the First Table of the Law tells you to do.
9. What should we pray for?
10. How can you learn to pray better?

Lesson 22

THY WILL BE DONE

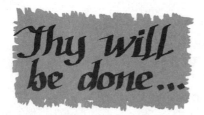

In our last regular lesson we learned what we should pray for. You will remember that Jesus taught His disciples how to pray; He gave them a pattern prayer—the Lord's Prayer. It is a perfect prayer. In just a few words it tells us the most important things we ought to pray for. In this lesson we are going to study one of the sentences in Jesus' perfect prayer.

How many times, do you think, have you prayed the Lord's Prayer? Many ministers pray it with you in church every Sunday. Often you pray it at meal times. You have probably prayed it a thousand times. A thousand times you have said to God, "Thy will be done, on earth as it is in heaven." Do you know what you are asking God when you pray those words?

What does "Thy will be done" mean?

When the family is planning a vacation, sometimes there is a problem. Some want to go swimming. Others want to go to a place where they can ride horseback or go fishing. When this happens, each boy or girl tries to get what he or she wants. Maybe you would say, "I want to go where we can swim." That is like saying, "I want *my will* to be done. I want us all to go where we can swim."

How did Jesus teach you to pray? Did He tell you to say, "*My* will be done"? No, He told you to say, "*Thy* will be done." That is a hard thing to pray, isn't it? We all want our own way. We all want our own will to be done. But the way we want things is not always the right way.

What are we asking God when we pray, "Thy will be done"?

When we pray to God, "Thy will be done," we are asking God to help us do three things. First, we are asking God to help us say "*No*" to our own will and "*Yes*" to God's will. For example, you pray at the breakfast table, "Thy will be done." Then you go off to school. All day you remember that you  asked God to help you say "*No*" to things that are wrong, such as cheating, disobeying the teacher, or being unkind to others. And you remember that you asked God to help you say "*Yes*" to the things that God wants you to do, such as being kind to others, and doing your best work.

Second, you are asking God to bless those things that are pleasing to Him. For example, you are asking Him to bless and help you in your studies. You are asking Him to bless and help your parents in their work, and to bless the church and everyone who does God's work.

Third, when you pray, "Thy will be done," you are asking God to help you become more like Jesus. He prayed, "Not my will, but thine, be done." Jesus said that He came into the world to do just one thing—the will of His heavenly Father. Jesus obeyed every one of God's commandments, and He did

the work that God gave Him to do. He did this even though it meant He had to die on the cross.

Why do we pray, "on earth as it is in heaven"?

Jesus prayed, "Thy will be done, on earth as it is in heaven." In heaven the angels do exactly what God asks them to do. They don't argue or try to get out of doing it. They do God's will cheerfully. So when you pray those words, you are asking God to help you obey and serve Him the way the angels do.

But it isn't easy to do God's will. We would rather do our own will. Moses had that problem too. You can read the story in Exodus, chapters three and four. When he was taking care of the sheep, God came to him and told him to go back to Egypt and lead the children of Israel out of captivity. But Moses didn't want to do God's will. He thought of several excuses. He said, "Why should I do it?" And, "King Pharaoh won't believe me." His last excuse was, "I can't speak well enough to talk to a king."

Each time that Moses made an excuse, God told him that He would help him and bless him. The book of Exodus tells us the rest of the wonderful story of how Moses, who did God's will, became a great leader of God's people, and how God blessed and helped him.

God called Moses, and He calls you too. God's will is that you do His work and obey His commandments. Ask yourself these questions: What does God want me to do with my life? How does He want me to serve Him? How can I be more obe-

156

dient to His commandments? When you pray, "Thy will be done, on earth as it is in heaven," you are asking God to help you answer those questions.

PRAYER

Our Father who art in heaven, hallowed be Thy name. Thy kingdom come. Thy will be done, on earth as it is in heaven. Teach me Thy will and help me to do it. Help me to say, "Not my will, but Thine be done." Bless everyone who is trying to do Thy will. In Jesus' name I pray, Amen.

BIBLE VERSE

Teach me to do thy will;
For thou art my God.

Psalm 143:10

THINKING IN BLACK-ON-WHITE

1. Why is the Lord's Prayer a perfect prayer?
2. What three things are you asking God to help you do when you pray, "Thy will be done"?
3. Who gives us the example of doing God's will perfectly? See John 6:38.
4. How can you learn what God's will is for you? Read Psalm 119:9-11.
5. What do we learn about doing God's will from the story of Moses in the book of Exodus, chapters three and four?

QUESTIONS AND ANSWERS FOR MEMORY WORK

1. **What is the will of God for you?**
   The will of God for me is to do His work and obey His commandments.

2. **What are you asking when you pray, "Thy will be done"?**
I am asking God to help me say "No" to my will and "Yes" to His will.

3. **Why do you pray, "On earth as it is in heaven"?**
I pray "On earth as it is in heaven," because I am asking God to help me obey His will perfectly as the angels in heaven do.

WHAT DO YOU THINK ABOUT IT?

When you pray, "Thy will be done," you are asking God to show you His will and to help you do it. Here are some problems you may face. In each one, what do you believe God's will would be?

1. School begins in twenty minutes. Your friends need you to even sides in a ball game. But you have some arithmetic problems that must be done before school begins.

2. You find fifty cents on the floor in the hall at school.

3. You earn ten dollars a month. What will you do with the money?

4. You cannot invite all of your classmates to your birthday party. There are too many. How would you decide which ones to invite and which ones to leave out?

THE KING'S OFFICERS

On the back of your church bulletin there may be a list of the elders and deacons of your church. In some churches they walk into the sanctuary and sit together in reserved seats. Those men, together with your minister, are the officers of your church. In this lesson we shall learn about those officers.

Sometimes the Bible compares the church of Jesus Christ to an army. But the church is different from a regular army. It does not fight with swords or guns. It uses the Word of God to fight against sin and to help people. The officers of the church are also different from the officers in an army.

Jesus Christ is the great King who leads His church. Even when He went back to heaven, He did not leave His church without leaders. If He had, His followers would be like an army without officers. So He commanded that officers be chosen to lead His people. But Jesus did not compare those leaders to military generals or captains. He compared them to shepherds who would take care of a flock of sheep.

Jesus said, "I am the good shepherd." All around the world He has flocks of believers. We call these flocks *congregations*. And for each flock Jesus calls an under-shepherd—a pastor— who leads the flock into the green pastures of God's truth and beside the still waters of His loving care. The name *pastor* means that the minister is called by Jesus to pasture the flock.

What are the duties of the pastor?

The pastor is a shepherd. It is his duty to be a good shepherd to his flock. The Bible tells us that a good shepherd does five things.

First, a good shepherd feeds his flock. He leads them into green pastures where they can eat and grow strong. This is the pastor's most important work. He doesn't feed his flock grass, but he feeds them with the Word of God. So he preaches on Sunday. He also teaches the Word in Bible classes and in other meetings. And he leads in the Lord's Supper and in Holy Baptism.

Second, a good shepherd takes special care of the weak and the sick ones in his flock. He carries the very young ones, the lame and the weak in his arms. So a pastor of a congregation visits the sick, the lonely and the sad ones in his flock. He comforts them and helps them by telling them about the wonderful promises God gives to those who follow Him. He listens to their problems and prays with them.

Third, a good shepherd keeps close track of each member of his flock. He watches for sore feet, running eyes, sharp burrs in the wool, and such things. So a pastor visits the members of his church. The elders do this with him. They visit each home to see that everyone is getting along well. They want to help those who are having

trouble. Some are having a hard time with sin. Others are having different kinds of problems. That is why they visit your home. They come to help you.

Fourth, a good shepherd keeps wolves and other enemies out of his flock. He carries a rod and a staff. And so the pastor, with his elders, keeps a close eye on the flock. Sometimes a person in the church does not lead a good life. Or someone may believe things that the Bible says are not true. Such people can lead others in the church into trouble. The

minister and the elders visit such a person and try to help him give up his wicked and wrong ways. They pray for such a person and show him what the Bible teaches.

Fifth, a good shepherd seeks for lost sheep. So the pastor looks for people who are not followers of Jesus. He visits people who do not go to church. He tells them the good news of how Jesus died to save sinners. And he invites them to come to church.

Sometimes people who are in the church will stop following Jesus. They wander off like the lost sheep in the parable. The minister and the elders visit such people and try to bring them back.

Have you ever thought how wonderful the work of a pastor is? Where do you think Jesus gets His under-shepherds? He calls them from among young people who are planning their lives. He calls them from among boys and girls like you.

What are the duties of the elders?

Elders are also chosen by Jesus to care for His flock. You have already seen that most of the things a pastor does are also done by the elders. The minister of a church works with the elders in doing the work of a good shepherd. The only thing the elders don't do is preach at the church services. They do help with the sacraments and serve the Lord's Supper.

The elders have one other duty. They must see that the pastor does his work well and leads a good Christian life.

What are the duties of the deacons?

Some of the most important work of the church is done by the deacons. They, too, are officers called by Christ. It is their duty to take care of the poor in the church. They help widows, orphans, sick people, those who can't find work, and all who are in need.

The deacons gather the gifts and offerings that God's people give and use these gifts to help those who are

in need. - In this way they show the love of Christ. You may read the story in Acts 6:1-6 of why and how the first deacons were called to do this work.

What are my duties to the officers of the church?

Jesus is the King of the church. The officers are His servants. Jesus gives the officers their authority. Their work is Jesus' work. There is no more important work in all the world.

If you love Jesus, then you will love His church and the officers of the church. The work of the officers is often very hard. Pray for them and show respect to them. They rule for Jesus.

PRAYER

Dear God, I thank Thee for the church where I worship Thee. I thank Thee for our minister and the elders and deacons. Please help them in their important work. And help me to be a good member of the church. In Jesus' name, Amen.

BIBLE VERSE

And he gave some to be apostles; and some, prophets; and some, evangelists; and some, pastors and teachers; for the perfecting of the saints.
Ephesians 4:11, 12a

THINKING IN BLACK-ON-WHITE

1. What are the five duties of the pastor?
2. What are the duties of the elders?
3. What are the duties of the deacons?

4. Where do the officers of the church get their authority (their right to rule)?

5. How does a church go about getting a minister? How does a church get its elders and deacons?

6. What is your duty to the officers of the church?

QUESTIONS AND ANSWERS FOR MEMORY WORK

1. **How does Jesus Christ govern His church?**
Jesus Christ governs His church through the officers of the church.

2. **Who are the officers of the church?**
The officers of the church are the ministers or pastors, elders and deacons.

3. **What are the main duties of the officers?**
The main duty of the pastor is to preach and teach, the duty of the elders is to rule, and the duty of the deacons is to do works of mercy.

WHAT DO YOU THINK ABOUT IT?

1. Tommy read in the church bulletin that the minister and an elder were going to visit his home on Wednesday afternoon at 4:30. This worried him. He tried to think of some way he could miss it. Maybe he would get sick. Or perhaps the school bus would break down and he would get home too late. Why do you think Tommy wanted to miss this visit?

2. How many of the following questions can you answer?
What are the names of the elders and deacons in your church?
What is a consistory or a council?
Why do the elders and deacons sit together in some churches?
If there were no minister around, who would lead the church services on Sunday?

CLAIMED BY GOD

One Sunday about ten or eleven years ago your parents held you in their arms and brought you to the front of church. There you were baptized. First the minister read about the meaning of baptism. Then he sprinkled water on your forehead and said, "[your name], I baptize you into the name of the Father and of the Son and of the Holy Spirit."

What happened to you when you were baptized? That is what this lesson is about.

Elsa and Connie were neighbors. They talked together about many things. One day Elsa asked Connie, "Were you baptized when you were a baby?"

Connie said she didn't know. Her parents had never said anything to her about it. But she was quite sure she had never been baptized, because her parents never went to church.

That evening Elsa asked her mother about it. "Mother, Connie says she was never baptized. Does that make her different from me?"

"Yes, Elsa, it does," answered her mother, "but you are different in ways that you can't always see."

This puzzled Elsa a little bit until her mother explained it. This explanation was not only for Elsa. Your parents would say the same thing. So this explanation is for you too.

Why did my parents have me baptized?

When you were born, your parents thanked God for giving you to them. They prayed that you would grow up to be a child of God. They trusted wonderful promises that God gives

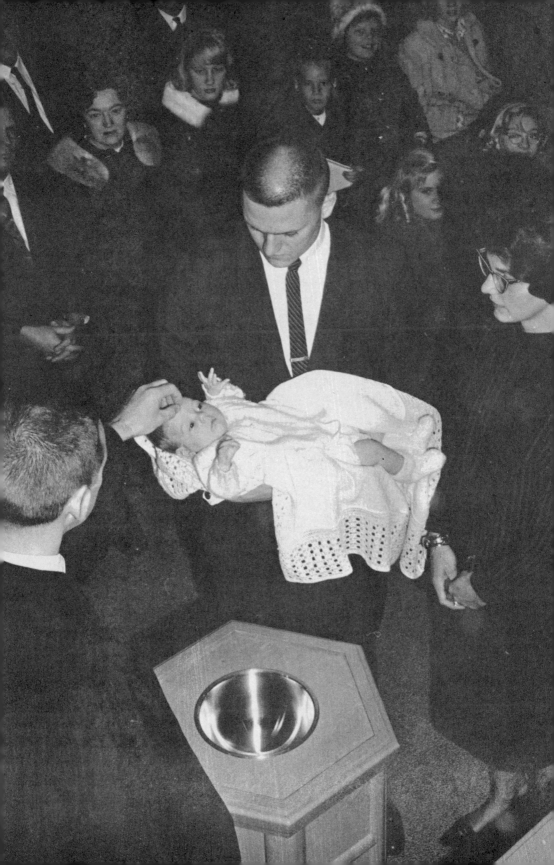

in the Bible for Christian fathers and mothers. God says, "I will be a God to you and to your children." In another place God says that the promise of salvation is to parents and to their children. This promise is God's covenant with us.

At baptism God speaks this promise to us. So when you were very small, your parents took you to church to be baptized. There the minister sprinkled water on your forehead, saying, "I baptize you into the name of the Father, and of the Son, and of the Holy Spirit."

Why did the minister sprinkle water on me?

The water that the minister sprinkled on you stands for the blood of Jesus Christ that washes away your sins. The water is a sign. Boys and girls sometimes use sign language, just as the Indians did. When an Indian raised his hand it meant that he came in peace. In the same way the water used in baptism is a sign from God. God says to your parents, "The water that is sprinkled on your child is a sign to you of My promise that I will wash away this child's sins with the blood of Jesus."

In some churches a little water is poured on the head of the child. In other churches the whole person is put under water. In our church we sprinkle the water. It is not important just how the water is used. The important thing is that we understand that the water is God's sign language. Just as the water washes away dirt, so God promises to wash away our sins with the blood of Jesus.

Why was I baptized into the name of the Father, Son and Holy Spirit?

You were baptized into the name of the Father, and of the Son, and of the Holy Spirit.

God the Father says to you, "I will keep the promise I made to your parents. I will be your God and will adopt you as my child. I will bless you."

God's Son, Jesus Christ, says to you, "My blood was shed that your sins might be forgiven."

And God, the Holy Spirit, says to you, "I will live in your heart and help you to live for God."

"You see, Elsa," her mother went on, "baptism does make you different. You are God's child. God has a claim on your life."

God has a claim on your life too.

The early pioneers went west, looking for new homes. When they found a good place to live they would stake a claim to the land that they wanted. When you were baptized God staked a claim to your life. This means that your life belongs to God.

There is a sad story about Esau in the Bible. One time he was very hungry. His brother Jacob said, "I will trade this bowl of food for your birthright." Esau agreed to this. His birthright was the good things he would some day receive from his father Isaac. Yet Esau traded away the wonderful promises and blessings that his father was going to give him. He did it just for a bowl of food. Would you do what Esau did?

God your Father has made wonderful promises to you. He has promised to be your God, to forgive your sins, and to give you everlasting life. What are you doing with God's promises —His covenant—with you? Are you trying to serve Him? Are you trying to obey His Word? If you are not, then you are like Esau.

When you were baptized, God made you a member of His church. When you are a little older you will want to stand up in church and say that you love God and that you want to serve Him. You were too small to do this when you were baptized. But soon you will be able to do this. We call this Public Profession of Faith.

PRAYER

Almighty God, I thank Thee for the promises that were given to me in my baptism. I thank Thee that I was Thy child even before I knew it. Help me now to live like Thy child, to love Thee and serve Thee. In Jesus' name I pray, Amen.

BIBLE VERSE

*For ye are all sons of God, through faith, in Christ
Jesus. For as many of you as were baptized into
Christ did put on Christ.*

Galatians 3:26, 27

THINKING IN BLACK-ON-WHITE

1. What does the water in baptism stand for?
2. Does it make any difference how the water is used in baptism? What is important?
3. Why were you baptized into the name of the Holy Trinity?
4. What promises does God make to you in your baptism?
5. What does God expect of you as a baptized child?

QUESTIONS AND ANSWERS FOR MEMORY WORK

1. **What is the meaning of baptism?**
Baptism means that God gives us a sign and a seal that He forgives our sins and receives us into His family.

2. **What sign does God give us in baptism?**
God gives us the sign of water, which stands for the blood of Jesus, by which we are cleansed from our sins.

3. **What must you do with your baptism?**
I must believe God's promise of salvation and show my thankfulness by loving and serving Him.

WHAT DO YOU THINK ABOUT IT?

1. Five babies were baptized in church one Sunday morning. Two of them cried and made a lot of noise. People could hardly hear what the minister said. When Peter got home he asked his parents why little babies have to be baptized in church. Why can't the minister come to the house? It would be so much easier. What do you think is the answer to Peter's question?

2. After Elsa's mother told her about baptism, Elsa felt sorry for Connie because she had not been baptized. She wondered whether Connie could be saved. Do you think Connie can be saved?

WHAT DOES THE LORD'S SUPPER MEAN?

Joey always went to church with his family. But four times a year the church service was different. On those Sundays the older people would celebrate the Lord's Supper. Joey would watch as his father and mother ate a little piece of bread and drank a little wine. Joey wondered what this meant. You have probably wondered about this too. Why do Christians eat bread and drink wine together? What does this mean? What do the bread and wine stand for? That is what this lesson is about.

As Joey was sitting there in church, he just couldn't wait to ask his questions. So he leaned over and asked his father, "May I have some too?" His father answered that he could when he became a little older. "Well, what is it all about?" asked Joey. "What does it mean?"

Joey was doing the right thing. The best way to learn about the Christian life is to ask questions. And the best people to ask are your parents. But Joey's father knew that he couldn't explain it very well while sitting there in church. So he told Joey to save his questions until they got home.

Why does our country have a flag?

"Now let's talk about your questions," said Joey's father when they came home and he sat down in his easy chair. Joey sat next to him on the footstool. "I don't get it," Joey started. "Why do we have the Lord's Supper in church?"

The rest of this lesson is what Joey's father told him.

Every country has a flag. On holidays people hang flags from their homes. We have flags in school. Flags fly from our government buildings. Do you know what a flag really is? It is more than just a piece of cloth. It is a sign of our country. It stands for the nation we live in. When we see our flag we think of our country.

The Lord's Supper is something like a flag. The bread and wine are signs that stand for the body and blood of Jesus. When we see these signs, we remember that Jesus died for us on the cross. Eating this bread and drinking this wine is one way of saying that we believe Jesus saves us from our sins.

What does the rainbow in the sky mean?

Do you remember what happened after the flood in Noah's day? The old world had been destroyed by water. Then God made a new beginning. At that time God promised that the world would never be destroyed by a flood again. Spring and summer, fall and winter would follow each other every year.

174

To prove His promise God gave a sign. He pointed to the beautiful rainbow in the sky and said, "Whenever you see this sign, you will be reminded of My promise. The rainbow stands for My promise."

You see, the Lord's Supper is something like the rainbow. The bread and the wine are signs that tell us what God has promised to do for us. God has promised to save us from our sins. This is why Jesus Christ died on the cross. The Lord's Supper always reminds us of Christ's death on the cross.

Why do people use seals on important papers?

Have you ever seen an important paper? Men sign their names on such papers to show that they agree with what the

paper says. Then a seal is stamped on this paper. The seal means that this agreement cannot be broken.

The Lord's Supper is also a seal. It is a seal that God has given so that we may never doubt His promises. The broken bread and the poured-out wine remind us that God will surely give us all the blessings that Jesus earned for us on the cross.

"So far we have learned two things about the Lord's Supper," Joey's father said. Let's try to remember them:

1. The bread and the wine are *signs* that point to the cross and remind us of God's promises and Christ's death for us.

2. The bread and the wine are *seals* by which God promises surely to give us all the blessings of Christ's great salvation.

Where did we get these signs and seals?
How were they given to us? Who gave them?

Joey always watched carefully as his minister broke the bread and handed out the wine. He wondered how this sacrament began. Did his minister think up this idea?

"The Lord's Supper was started by Jesus in the Upper Room," Joey's father explained. "The night before Jesus died on the cross, He celebrated the first Lord's Supper with His disciples. At that time our Lord commanded that Christians everywhere should celebrate this Supper as a way to remember His death. Matthew tells us about it in the Bible: 'As they were eating, Jesus took bread, and blessed, and brake it; and he gave to the disciples, and said, Take, eat; this is my body.

And he took a cup, and gave thanks, and gave to them, saying, Drink ye all of it; for this is my blood of the covenant, which is poured out for many unto remission of sins' (Matthew 26: 26, 27). One day you too can obey this command of Jesus by joining us at the Lord's Supper."

Joey liked this idea. But he had one more question.

*What does going to the Lord's Supper
mean for us?*

"At the Lord's Supper Christ is our Host," Joey's father explained, "and we are His guests. Eating the bread and drinking the wine mean much to us as Christians," he said, "but let us mention just four things.

"First, by eating this bread and drinking this wine we show that we believe in Jesus as our Savior.

"Second, at the Lord's Supper Jesus makes us very sure that we are children of God and that our heavenly Father forgives all our sins.

"Third, through this sacrament Jesus makes us stronger Christians.

"Finally, by obeying Jesus' command to remember His death, we as Christians promise to give our lives to Him."

When Father finished, Joey said he understood much better than before what the bread and the wine mean. From that time on he really looked forward to the time when he would go to the Lord's Supper just as his father and mother did. Maybe you feel the same way about it.

PRAYER

Father in heaven, I thank Thee for giving Thy Son to be my Savior. I thank Thee for the Lord's Supper, which shows clearly Thy great love for me. Help me to be sure that I am Thy child. Make my faith stronger. Lead me step by step until one day I may join other Christians at the Lord's Supper. This I pray in remembrance of Jesus' death, Amen.

BIBLE VERSE

As they were eating, Jesus took bread, and blessed, and brake it; and he gave to the disciples, and said, Take, eat; this is my body. And he took a cup, and gave thanks, and gave to them, saying, Drink ye all of it; for this is my blood of the covenant, which is poured out for many unto remission of sins.

Matthew 26:26-28

THINKING IN BLACK-ON-WHITE

1. What does the Bible say about children learning from their parents, as Joey did from his father? Read Joshua 4:5-7.

2. Tell how the bread and wine of the Lord's Supper are like the flag of your country.

3. Tell how the signs of bread and wine in the Lord's Supper are like the sign of the rainbow.

4. Tell how the bread and wine of the Lord's Supper are like seals on important papers.

5. Pretend that you had been at the first Lord's Supper, and someone asked you what was the most important thing that happened there. What would you say?

6. What meaning does the Lord's Supper have for Christians today?

QUESTIONS AND ANSWERS FOR MEMORY WORK

1. **Why are the bread and the wine of the Lord's Supper called signs?**

The bread and the wine of the Lord's Supper are called signs because they point to Jesus' death on the cross and remind us of His great love for sinners.

2. **Why are the bread and the wine of the Lord's Supper called seals?**

The bread and the wine of the Lord's Supper are called seals because, through them, God promises surely to give us all the blessings of Christ's great salvation.

3. **How did the Lord's Supper begin?**

The Lord's Supper began when Christ held the first Lord's Supper with His disciples in the upper room just before His death.

4. **Why do we still celebrate the Lord's Supper?**

We still celebrate the Lord's Supper because Christ commanded us to do this in remembrance of Him.

5. **What does taking the Lord's Supper mean for us?**

By taking the Lord's Supper we show that we believe in Jesus as our Savior and that we need Him to strengthen our lives.

WHAT DO YOU THINK ABOUT IT?

1. Louise was playing church with some of her friends. "Let's have the Lord's Supper too," she said. "Okay," said Mary, "but I don't understand what it is all about. What does the Lord's Supper mean?" If you were Louise, how would you explain the meaning of the Lord's Supper?

2. After Louise finished telling Mary about the Lord's Supper, they all continued playing church. They pretended they were having the Lord's Supper. Just then Louise's brother Dale came in and joined in their game. "I always wanted to go to the real Lord's Supper," Dale said. "I can hardly wait until I can really go." Louise told Dale this was wrong, because the Lord's Supper is only for older people, and it is wrong for boys and girls to want to go to the Lord's Supper. Was she right?

WHAT HAPPENS WHEN WE DIE?

Everybody at school knew Nick Horley. He was in the fifth grade. Like all other boys his age, Nick was naughty sometimes, but still he loved Jesus and tried to live as a Christian. One day Nick became very sick. A few days later the teacher told the class that Nick had died. All the boys and girls were very sad. They wondered what happens when a person dies. What really happened to Nick? Where is he now? What is he doing? So the teacher talked to the class about what happens when we die. That is what this lesson is about.

Like everybody else, little Nick Horley knew that someday he would die. But in his life it came quite soon. When the time came, he was ready. He cheered up his parents. He told them not to cry a lot. They could be happy, too, he said, because he was going to live with Jesus. His parents were glad to hear this. They knew he would have a perfect life in the Father's home in heaven.

Then came the funeral. Nick's class was there. The minister gave a short message. What he said about heaven cheered everyone. Then they went to the cemetery. Just a little way off the narrow gravel road they buried Nick Horley. Then everybody went home.

Back in school the next week some of the children wondered just where Nick was now. Was he in heaven? Or was he in the grave?

So the teacher talked about these questions again.

What happens to our body when we die?

We are made up of two parts, the teacher explained. One part of us we can see—we call this our body. The other part of us we cannot see, but it is just as real as our body—we call this our soul. The soul is that self inside of us that makes us what we are; it is our real self. If we are Christians, then our whole self, both body and soul, belongs to Jesus.

During our life body and soul live together in one person. But this changes when we die. Then our body and our soul are separated from each other. No one really knows what this is like. But the Bible does tell us the most important things we must know about dying.

When we die, our body falls asleep for a long time. It is no longer alive. It can't move anymore. It can't think or talk. Our body isn't much good to us this way. So we lay it to rest in the grave. Our body remains in the grave until Jesus comes back to earth again. Then He will raise our bodies from the grave, and make them alive again, just as He arose on Easter Sunday.

What happens to our soul when we die?

At the end of our life here on earth our soul does not die, as our body does. Our soul lives on forever. When we die, our soul says good-bye to our body for a while. Right at that moment our soul goes directly to heaven. We don't have to wait a single day. Remember what Jesus said to the thief on the cross, the one who believed in Him, "Today thou shalt be with me in paradise" (Luke 23:43).

This is the wonderful future of every child of God. That is why Nick's classmates and his parents could smile even through their tears. Even though Nick was no longer with them, they could be happy to know that he was now with Jesus in heaven. That is why, as the teacher said, no Christian has to be afraid of dying. For death is like moving from one place to another, from our home on earth to the mansions in heaven that Jesus is preparing for us (John 14:2).

> *Will everybody go to heaven? Why will some people go to hell? What decides whether we will go to heaven or to hell?*

Right now we must decide to trust in Jesus. For unless we live for Jesus now, we cannot live with Him in heaven after we die.

All men must die—those who are not Christians too. Their bodies are also buried, and their souls also live on forever. But instead of going to heaven, those who do not believe in Jesus will go to hell. Hell is a dreadful place, because it is a place of separation from God. And there will be no second chance to decide about Jesus after this life. That is why our life now is so important. That's why today is important.

Jesus teaches these truths very clearly in the parable of the rich man and Lazarus. Read this parable in Luke 16:19-31. What we do about Jesus now decides what our life will be like in the future. In many ways Lazarus was a very poor man, but he had that one thing that is all-important. He believed in God. The rich man had everything except that one most important thing. This explains why the one man went to heaven and the other man to hell. During this life we must decide for or against Jesus. We cannot change things after we die.

What kind of life will we have in heaven?

The boys and girls in the fifth grade wondered what kind of life Nick now had in heaven. The teacher told them as much as she could about how we shall live in heaven. But she couldn't tell the whole story. It is even better than the best we can imagine. It is so wonderful that even the Bible can't tell us everything about it. But God has told us what we need to know.

When our body dies on earth, our soul will awake in heaven. Then we will see Jesus face to face. We will sing the song of salvation. Sin will be forever past. There will be no more sickness or sadness. We will never again be angry or afraid. Every day there will be new and wonderful things to do and new and wonderful ways to praise God.

There is one more great chapter in this glorious story of salvation. But for that we will have to wait until next week.

PRAYER

Lord Jesus, I am glad to know that Thou art my King both in life and in death. I thank Thee for helping me live as a Christian today. When I die, may I live with Thee in heaven forever. Help me to use both my body and my soul in serving Thee, so that this wonderful life on earth may one day lead to the perfect life in heaven. Amen.

BIBLE VERSE

We are of good courage, I say, and are willing rather to be absent from the body, and to be at home with the Lord.

II Corinthians 5:8

THINKING IN BLACK-ON-WHITE

1. Why was it good for Nick Horley's class to be at the funeral?

2. What happens to our bodies when we die? Read II Corinthians 5:8 and Ecclesiastes 12:7.
3. What happens to our souls when we die? See Philippians 1:23.
4. Why will some people go to hell instead of to heaven?
5. Can we decide to believe in Jesus after we die?

QUESTIONS AND ANSWERS FOR MEMORY WORK
1. **What is death?**
Death is moving from this life to eternal life.
2. **What happens when we die?**
When we die, our bodies are laid to rest in the grave and our souls go directly to live with Jesus in heaven.
3. **Who will go to heaven?**
Those who believe in Jesus will go to heaven, but those who do not believe in Jesus will go to hell.
4. **What is heaven?**
Heaven is the wonderful place that Jesus is preparing for all His people, where we shall live with Him in glory forever.

WHAT DO YOU THINK ABOUT IT?
1. Ted was one of the boys in Nick's class. Nick and he often played together at school. Sometimes they walked home together. So Ted was very sad when Nick died, especially after the funeral. He kept on saying, "Poor Nick, poor little Nick." Ted's mother said he should feel sad for Nick's parents, but there was no need to feel sorry for Nick. What do you suppose she meant by that?
2. Once there was a boy who knew about Jesus very well. He knew that Jesus wants us to believe in Him right now. But this boy thought he would just wait a while, because he was still young. He told himself there would be lots of time to decide about Jesus after he got older. Do you think this boy was doing the right thing?

THE LAST DAY

At the end of our last lesson we made a promise. Do you remember? We said that there is one more great chapter in the wonderful true story of salvation. Now in this lesson we must keep that promise. This chapter is about the happy ending of the Christian life. It is a chapter that really only God can write. For it tells about things that will happen in the future. But God has told us some of the most important things about it in the Bible. So let's learn now what will happen to us when Jesus comes back to earth.

When will that great day come?

The owner of a little grocery store kept this sign in his window: "Live every day as though Christ had died yesterday, arisen this morning, and were returning tomorrow."

As Christians we can look backward with thanks to Good Friday, when Jesus died, and to Easter Sunday, when He arose. But we can also look forward with hope to His return on the Last Day. What a wonderful day of glorious miracles that will be!

But when will that great day come? Jesus said, "No man knows the day or the hour." Only God knows this secret. He has a set time. When all God's plans for the world are worked out, then He will send His Son into the world for the second time. But He has not told us the exact day, because He wants us always to live as though it could happen today.

Jesus told us that we must watch and pray and live for His return. Otherwise that great day will come upon us as a thief in the night. You know how a thief comes. He breaks in when you least expect it. So Jesus warns us not to be caught sleeping, as the five foolish virgins in one of His parables, but to be ready for His return, as the five wise virgins. Would you be ready if Jesus came today?

What will happen to us on that great day?

Because of sin, the world is full of troubles. We have the problems of sickness and crime and race hatred and war and many other problems. The Bible says that, near the end of time, our troubles will become so great that men will not be able to live in peace with each other. It will be very hard to be a Christian. Wicked men will persecute us. People will give up all hope of having a good life. Then Jesus will return. He is the only one who can save us from all our troubles.

When Jesus appears upon the clouds of heaven, suddenly everything will be changed. Wickedness will be destroyed. With the help of the mighty angels, King Jesus will make the world perfect again—perfect as it was before sin entered the world. Satan and his wicked angels, all people who hate God, and everything sinful will be defeated and locked up in hell forever.

If we are living when Jesus comes back we will be changed. We will not die. But in a moment, in the twinkling of an eye, Jesus will change our bodies into glorified bodies, like His own. We will never again become sick or get hurt or die. Jesus will also make our souls pure, so that we will never again think or say or do anything bad. Then we will be holy, completely perfect, so that we can live with God and the holy angels forever in the new heaven and the new earth.

186

*What will happen to Christians who
have already died?*

In the days of the Apostle Paul many Christians thought
they would still be living when Jesus comes back. They felt
sorry for their dear ones who had already died because they
thought their dear ones would miss the great and wonderful
day of Jesus' return. Paul told them, in one of his letters, that
there was no reason to fear this. Then he explained how things
will happen on that great day.

We learned last week that when Christians die their bodies
are buried, but immediately their souls go to live with Jesus
in heaven. When Jesus comes back He will take with Him
the souls of those in heaven, so that they too will share in His
victory. He will first raise from the grave the bodies of those
who have died. But these bodies will be glorified—just as Jesus'
body was glorified when He arose from the dead. There will
be a happy reunion of all who are still alive with those who
have already died. Then we shall all live with Jesus forever.

*What will happen to unbelievers when
Jesus returns?*

For people who hate God, that last day will be most terrible.
Unbelievers who are still alive will meet Jesus with great fear.
The bodies of unbelievers who have already died will also be
raised from the grave and be united with their souls; but their
bodies will not be glorified. Then Jesus the Judge will say to
them, "Go away from Me forever, you lovers of evil. Because
you rejected Me, I will reject you now. Enter into the everlasting punishment of hell."

Hell is a place of living death. Jesus said that the worm
never dies there, and the fires always burn. The everlasting
punishment of hell is separation from God. Where God is not
there is no love—for God is love. Where God is not there is

no light—for God is light. In hell the fire of God's anger burns forever against the terrible sin of unbelief.

Heaven is just the opposite of hell. In heaven there is love and light and friendship because God is there. God will wipe away all our tears, and there will be no more trouble or evil or sickness or pain. In work and play we will show how thankful we are because God saved us from our sins and brought us to heaven to live with Him. Living in heaven means being with the family of our heavenly Father forever. Who could ask for more? Pray Jesus to lead you to that heavenly home.

PRAYER

Father in heaven, Thou knowest the day when Jesus will come to earth again. I do not ask to know the time. Help me always to be ready, so that, when that great day comes, I may belong to Thy great family in heaven forever. Lord Jesus, lead me step by step to Thy heavenly home. Holy Spirit, help me to begin living the life of heaven every day while I live here on earth. In Jesus' name, Amen.

BIBLE VERSE

The hour cometh, in which all that are in the tombs shall hear his voice, and shall come forth; they that have done good, unto the resurrection of life; and they that have done evil, unto the resurrection of judgment.
John 5:28-29.

THINKING IN BLACK-ON-WHITE

1. What does the Bible teach us about the time Jesus will come back to earth again?
2. How must we get ready for Jesus' return?
3. When Jesus comes again, what will happen to those who are living and to those who have already died? Read I Thessalonians 4:13-18.

4. What is the difference between heaven and hell?

5. How must we live now if we wish to live in God's great family in heaven forever?

QUESTIONS AND ANSWERS FOR MEMORY WORK

1. **When will Jesus come to earth again?**

   Jesus will come again on the last day.

2. **Do we know when the last day will come?**

   We do not know when the last day will come, but we should always live as though it could happen today.

3. **What will happen to us if we are still alive when Jesus comes again?**

   If we are alive when Jesus comes again, He will make our souls perfect and glorify our bodies, so that we can live with Him in glory forever.

4. **When Jesus comes again, what will He do for Christians who have already died?**

   When Jesus comes again, He will raise the dead from the grave so that, with glorified bodies and perfect souls, they may live with Him in glory forever.

WHAT DO YOU THINK ABOUT IT?

1. Some people say, "I am going to live just as I please until a little while before Jesus comes back. Then I will start living a good life." Is this a good way to live?

2. Do you remember Nick Horley, the boy who died? We talked about him in our last lesson. Well, the teacher was talking to the class about what will happen on the last day. Nick's good friend, Ted, wondered whether Nick would still know him when they got to heaven. The teacher said, "I think so." "Then," Ted replied, "I will tell him all about what happened at school after he left." What do you think about this idea?

Lesson 28

LORD, I BELIEVE

A Review Lesson

We have reached the end of the road in our travels through this book. Our last lesson was about the end of that road. It ends in heaven for those who believed in Jesus Christ. It ends in hell for those who did not believe.

This book shows you the way to heaven. If you can say with all your heart, "Lord, I believe," then you are on the road to heaven. The last six lessons have told you how you should walk the road to heaven. You may be sure that God helps you as you walk this road.

First, we must pray, "Thy will be done, on earth as it is in heaven." We must ask God to help us say "No" to what is wrong and to say "Yes" to His will. If we obey God's commandments, then we will not slip off the road of Christian living.

We don't walk the road alone. All the members of the church of Jesus Christ travel with us. Christ is our Shepherd. He leads us. Jesus also calls pastors, elders and deacons to lead His people. They help us in many ways.

As we walk this road, we know that we are God's children. We know that our sins are forgiven. God has given us the sign of baptism. And He has a claim on our lives. We do not belong to ourselves; we belong to Jesus; we must serve Him.

We have another sign to help us. Jesus has given us the Lord's Supper. At the Lord's Supper we receive signs and seals to show that Jesus suffered and died for us. When you are old enough to make a public profession of your faith, then you too will eat the bread and drink the wine. It will strengthen your faith as you walk the road.

One day we shall reach the end of the road on this earth. If you have said, "Lord, I believe," and if you have served Him, then your soul will go to heaven to be with Jesus. Or Jesus may come back before that day. Then, too, you will be with Him.

When Jesus returns He will judge every person who has ever lived. Those who didn't love and serve Him will be cast from His presence into never-ending suffering of hell. But those who loved Him and served Him will live with Him forever in the new heaven and the new earth.

It is important to know the road to eternal life. This is God's way and we must walk in it. As long as you live you should pray, "Teach me Thy way." If you pray this sincerely you will want to know more about God's way. As you continue to study the Bible, you will see more clearly that God's way is wonderful. It is the only way to eternal life.

PRAYER

Dear heavenly Father, I thank Thee that I am Thy child. I thank Thee for my Christian parents and for our church where I have been taught the way of salvation. Help me to walk by faith as Thy obedient child until I meet Jesus, my Savior, face to face. In His name I pray, Amen.

REVIEW QUESTIONS

1. What are you asking of God when you pray, "Thy will be done, on earth as it is in heaven"?
2. How can you know what God's will is for you?
3. What are the duties of the pastor, the elders and the deacons?
4. Where do these church officers get their authority?
5. What does the water used in baptism stand for?

6. What does God expect of you as a baptized child?

7. What do we remember when we celebrate the Lord's Supper?

8. Why are the bread and the wine of the Lord's Supper called signs and seals?

9. What meaning does the Lord's Supper have for Christians today?

10. What happens to us when we die?

11. Will all men go to heaven when they die? Who only will go to heaven?

12. When will Jesus come back to earth?

13. What will Jesus do when He returns?

14. How should we live in order to get ready for the last day?